A Day in the Season of the Los Angeles Dodgers

A Day in the Season
of the
Los Angeles Dodgers

Photography and Text
by
Tom Zimmerman

SHAPOLSKY PUBLISHERS
NEW YORK

A Shapolsky Book

Copyright © 1990 by Tom Zimmerman

For any additional information, contact:
Shapolsky Publishers, Inc.
136 West 22nd Street, NY, NY 10011

1 2 3 4 5 6 7 8 9 10

Library of Congress Cataloging-in-Publication Data

Zimmerman, Tom, 1949–
A day in the season of the Los Angeles Dodgers
p.   cm.
ISBN 0-944007-89-9
1. Los Angeles Dodgers (Baseball team) 2. Baseball players—
United States—Biography. I. Title.
GV875.L6Z52   1990   796.357′64′0979494—dc20
90-32400   CIP

Book Design and Typography by
The Bartlett Press, Inc., Somerset, New Jersey

For Nancy – and all the innings yet to come

Orel Hershiser, Cy Young Award winner, 1988

CONTENTS

ACKNOWLEDGMENTS

A *Day in the Season of the Los Angeles Dodgers* started out as a series of articles for the *Los Angeles Downtown News*. Editor Marc Porter Zasada gave me free rein to pursue the story as I saw fit, and has my eternal gratitude.

The Dodgers have been extremely helpful in giving me access both to information and their stadium. Mike Williams arranged for clearance to the park, Ruth Ruiz helped set up interviews, Brent Shyer helped with ideas and to correct the manuscript, and Michael Vizvary, who is more adroit at doing three things at once than anyone I've ever met, always managed to track down even the most arcane piece of information. As is evident from the book, the entire Dodger operation, from the players to the cleanup crew, was always willing to put up with one more guy asking them questions. There would have been no book without their assistance.

Anyone who knows Nancy Newman Work appreciates her wonderful design sense. I am fortunate to know her very well and to have been the grateful recipient of her insight, trust, and cheerleading. She's even trying to become a baseball fan as I work on my appreciation of her candleholders.

The book was also helped by the encouragement and suggestions of Michael John Sullivan. He was always ready to give a supportive word when one was most needed. He introduced me to publisher Ian Shapolsky, whose immediate interest in the project resulted in the book you hold in your hands. Thanks also to Andy Dowdy for years of literary criticism.

My historical training came through the good offices of Anthony Turhollow, Norris Hundley, and Thomas Hines. I could not have asked for a better trio of stimulating educators. My father, Pius Zimmerman, first taught me how to use a camera and how to make photographic prints. My brother, Paul, and T.G. Lane, Larry Calderon, Lee Romero, and Mike Tandy (owner of the legendary Art Craft Rental Darkroom) all helped expand on my father's early lessons. My representative, Rachel Lozzi, who grew up with a Dodger pennant hanging on her wall, has been both insightfully critical and thoroughly supportive.

Finally, I want to thank Sr. Colette McManus for twelve years of Job-like patience.

Tom Zimmerman
Los Angeles
1990

Tommy Lasorda and Fred Claire, 1989

FOREWORD

A Day in the Season of the Los Angeles Dodgers celebrates time spent at Dodger Stadium. It wanders from the field to vendor's booths, stopping along the way for a hot dog and a chat with some ushers. The baseball day starts with the timeless echoing sound of a wooden bat hitting a ball in an empty stadium. It ends with the high-pitched whine of air blowers cleaning the place up after tens of thousands of people have passed through and gone.

Another part of the story is the Dodger organization. Its competence is legend throughout professional sports. In the 31 seasons since the team came west, five world championship pennants have fluttered in the center-field breeze. There have been twelve first-place finishes and nine second-place. Fallow periods are not indulged. Minor leaguers graduate to the majors, trades are made, free agents acquired. The team is never long out of contention.

But baseball is far more than just a sport or business venture. Professional athletics, like other forms of popular culture, tell us a great deal about the society that supports them. The reaction of Los Angeles fans to Kirk Gibson and his aggressiveness offers insights into that most misunderstood of cities. Perceptions of Dodger manager Tommy Lasorda are indicative of the role expectations assigned to American men. The autograph seekers around the players' parking lot after the game are part of the nationwide yearning to play some sort of role in the lives of the nation's idols. *A Day in the Season* grew out of a series of articles for the *Los Angeles Downtown News* and a small book called *Working at the Stadium*. Both the earlier works covered the triumphal 1988 season. The present volume expands the story through the less successful 1989 campaign. All of the photographs in the text are dated, so it is easy to tell which of the seasons the picture and caption cover.

They certainly were two very different years. The team changed. Steve Sax went to the Yankees, Danny Heep to the Red Sox. Eddie Murray and Willie Randolph came to the Dodgers from the American League. Kirk Gibson, the National League's Most Valuable Player in 1988, was on the disabled list much of 1989. Orel Hershiser went from setting a major league record by pitching 59 consecutive scoreless innings to suffering through a stretch of 34 innings where his team could not score a single run for him. One year, victors in the Fall Classic. The next, a constant struggle to leave the second division. One year where everything seemed to fall in for the Dodgers and a second year full of excellent pitching with no timely hitting. When asked about the difference between the two seasons, manager Tommy Lasorda commented, "Do you know we left over a thousand men on base? A thousand. You can't win anything playing like that."

Whether the team is winning or losing, the business of baseball continues. Fred Claire has to think of new ways to strengthen the team. Brent Shyer will be busy planning the next issue of the monthly *Dodgers Magazine*. Sam Fernandez is looking out for the team's legal interests. Annette Saldano is running her food stand on Field Level. Rick Foreman is selling ice cream in the pavilions. Don Buschhoff is hawking scorecards near the entrance to the stadium. All this activity is, of course, supported by fans who come to the park by the millions each season, and by those who turn their radios and televisions to the Dodgers game when the team plays. Different people are doing the same thing in every major league ballpark on any day of the season. I chose to examine how they are carried out at Dodger Stadium because it is the home of the team I grew up with. The arrival of the Dodgers in Los Angeles for the 1958 season is one of the fondest memories of my childhood and I have followed them devotedly ever since. Like most other fans, the idea of hanging around the stadium talking to the people who make it operate and play in it held enormous appeal. Not just for the sake of satisfying my curiosity about how the place gets cleaned up at night, but for giving me the chance to think about what baseball can tell us about American society in the late 20th century.

INTRODUCTION:
A LOS ANGELES BASEBALL HISTORY

Some Hollywood Stars celebrate winning the championship, 1952
(Courtesy, Florence Haney)

The Los Angeles Dodgers have been a wildly successful franchise. The main reason for this is the nature of the organization. Poor team showing has always brought shakeups. Not in management, but on the field where it will do some good. One family has owned the team since it left Brooklyn. The ballpark is scrupulously tended. All these are major factors in running a prosperous organization. But it should not be forgotten that the Dodgers were the beneficiary of a long tradition of support for professional baseball by Los Angeles fans.

The dust was just settling from the first of Los Angeles' many real estate booms when the city fielded its first professional baseball team. It was the late 1880s, and the streets were only just starting to be paved in the obscure town in Southern California. The team was a part of the outlaw California League – a circuit that was not recognized by the National Association of Professional Baseball Clubs. Home games were played at Praeger and Chutes Parks. They were part of a large amusement center located south of downtown where Hill Street dead-ended into Washington Boulevard. The 19th-century team's chief claims to fame are a night game played in 1893 which was lit by 20 kerosene lamps suspended on wires between poles, and that future evangelist Billy Sunday was a starting center fielder.

PACIFIC COAST LEAGUE

Organized baseball first came to Los Angeles when the Pacific Coast League opened for business in 1903. The city's entry was called the Angels, and would remain one of the mainstays of the Triple-A League until the Dodgers came west in 1958. The Angels' first seasons were played at Chutes Park, later switching to nearby Washington Park.

Former Coast League great Jimmie Rese, currently entering his 67th year in professional baseball as a coach with the California Angels, played in Washington Park as a second baseman with the Oakland Oaks. He remembers it as a typical minor league ballpark of its time. All the fencing and the single-tiered grandstand were made of wood. If you threw in the standing room, there was a capacity of maybe 15,000 fans.

The Angels were one of the mainstays of the P.C.L. for the next half century. The second local entry in the league has a much more traveled history. The team started life as the Vernon Tigers in 1909 when the P.C.L. expanded to accommodate a Sacramento franchise. The Tigers represented Vernon from 1909 to 1912 and again from 1915 to 1925. The two missing years were spent in Venice. After sixteen years of marginal success, the team moved north to join the Seals in San Francisco, changing their name to the Missions. Thirteen years later, after being the second team in a major city again, the Missions came back to Los Angeles as the second edition of the Hollywood Stars. In a foreshadowing of the Dodgers in 1958, the "Twinks" (as in "Twinkle, Twinkle, Little Star") played their first season at Gilmore Stadium, a converted football field.

WRIGLEY FIELD

In 1921, William Wrigley, Jr., who owned a chewing gum company, most of the Chicago Cubs, and all of Santa Catalina Island, bought the Los Angeles Angels from Johnny Powers. He soon found himself at odds with the city government. Mirroring a similar dilemma that would confront Walter O'Malley in Brooklyn some 35 years later, Wrigley argued that his team's fans could not reach the ballpark by car since parking was so inadequate. Washington Park was primarily served by streetcars, and in 1921 Angelenos were already deeply engrossed in their continuing affair with the automobile. Wrigley wanted to put in underground parking. The city said no, so he decided to move.

Land was purchased south of the city's center at 42nd and Avalon Boulevard, and the nation's second Wrigley Field was constructed. The Los Angeles version was a slightly scaled down version of the original in Chicago. Like its eastern counterpart it was easily reached by interurban train and the ball carried well when the wind was blowing out. The brick outfield wall was lightly covered with ivy and there was a small center-field bleacher section under a huge scoreboard.

There were a few differences. This was Southern California in the early 1920s, after all. Tile covered the roof of both the grandstand and the office tower, and palm trees grew just beyond the outfield fences. The dimensions were somewhat smaller than the major league park. Angel batters were faced with 340-foot foul lines and a center-field wall 412 feet away. But the power alleys were only 345 feet. These friendly dimensions helped make the western edition as much a paradise for fans of offensive baseball as its eastern counterpart. One very large difference existed between the two Wrigley Fields. Lights for night games were added in Los Angeles in 1930.

Wrigley Field was officially unveiled on September 29, 1925. The Commissioner of Baseball, Judge Kenesaw Mountain Landis, took the train west to officiate at the ceremonies. The ballpark, like its two-year-old neighbor, the Coliseum, was dedicated as a memorial to America's veterans of the First World War. The chewing gum magnate spared no expense in making the stadium the class act of the Pacific Coast League. Wrigley Field was the only venue in the

Wrigley Field, c. 1930

Wrigley Field, c. 1930

circuit that had a concrete grandstand until Seals Stadium opened in San Francisco six years later. Jimmie Reese did not see a better place to play ball until he went up to the New York Yankees in 1930.

Some great baseball was played at Wrigley over the years. The field was in almost continuous use during the season once the Angels were joined at the park from 1926 to 1935 by the first edition of the Hollywood Stars. Two legendary California natives sharpened their skills here before their inevitable graduation to the majors. San Francisco's Joe DiMaggio went right from the sandlots to AAA play with the Seals before going on to the Yankees. Ted Williams went directly from Hoover High School in San Diego to the P.C.L. Padres and quickly on to the Red Sox.

Such stellar players obviously brought fans to the ballparks, but the backbone of the league was the players who excelled at the AAA level but never quite made it into the big leagues. Two Angels are prominent in this category. Jigger Statz played center field for the Angels in the 1920s and '30s. He holds the Coast League records for most putouts, assists, chances accepted, and season fielding percentage. Steve Bilko came to the Angels in the mid-1950s after several seasons with the St. Louis Browns and Cardinals. Wrigley Field could have been built with Bilko in mind. He hit 55 home runs in 1956 and 56 home runs in 1957, giving Angel fans something to cheer about in the team's final two seasons.

Wrigley Field was one of the larger parks in the P.C.L. and could accommodate 22,00 fans. This generally provided far more seats than were necessary. Former usher Bill Fitzgerald remembers counting 136 people in the park one cold day in 1947. But even the bleachers would swell with fans for important games such as the League Championship series or contests with crosstown rivals, the Hollywood Stars.

Another sure filler of chairs was the arrival of major league barnstormers. Such teams came by in October and November after the close of the big league season. Teams would usually be led by a name star – such as Ty Cobb, Rogers Hornsby, Babe Ruth, or Bob Feller – and would consist of players from various major or AAA teams who wanted to make some extra money in the days when even a major leaguer needed a second job to make ends meet. The competition was keen and the crowds large whenever big league stars came to Los Angeles, but never more so than when one of the teams was made up of stars from the Negro Leagues. Satchel Paige often headed these teams of players who were barred from participation in "organized" baseball because of race until Branch Rickey signed Jackie Robinson to play for the Dodgers' Montreal farm club in 1946.

Both Wrigley Field and the Angels were purchased by the Brooklyn Dodgers in 1956. After officially agreeing to move west in 1957, the major league team set up its offices at Wrigley. The Giants played their home games at Seals Stadium in San Francisco until the unfortunate Candlestick Park opened in 1961, but Wrigley was deemed too small for major league play by Dodger brass. So the team played at the jerry-rigged Coliseum for the next four years.

No professional teams played at Wrigley between 1958 and 1960, but the old park did show up periodically on television. Both "Home Run Derby" and "The Mighty Casey" episode from *The Twilight Zone* were filmed there. In 1961, an American League expansion team, called appropriately the Los Angeles Angels, played its first season at Wrigley Field. But the following year the team moved to Dodger Stadium, which they called Chavez Ravine Stadium, while their own ballpark was being built in Anaheim. In 1966 the team went south to become the California Angels.

With its Pacific Coast League team in Spokane and its American League team in Anaheim, Wrigley Field's days were numbered. After several years of hosting softball leagues and traveling carnivals, Wrigley Field was dismantled. Gilbert Lindsay Park now occupies the old corner at 42nd and Avalon.

GILMORE FIELD

When Bob Cobb, president of the Brown Derby Restaurants, led a group bid to buy the Hollywood club from San Francisco beer baron Herbert Fleischaker in 1938, he was determined to give the Stars a home park separate from Wrigley Field. In order to raise the necessary capital to build the new stadium on Gilmore Island at Beverly and Fairfax, and pay operating expenses, Cobb sold blocks of stock in the club. Among the takers were several people prominent in Hollywood's chief local industry. Gary Cooper, George Raft, Robert Taylor, Barbara Stanwyck, Cecil B. DeMille, Bing Crosby, George Burns, Gracie Allen, and William Powell all had a piece of the club. This close association with Hollywood celebrities would be one of the lasting hallmarks of Gilmore Field.

The new home of the Hollywood Stars was a more traditional minor league park than Wrigley. It had a wooden grandstand with seating for 12,987 fans. Eucalyptus trees sprouted behind the advertisement-covered outfield fence, not bleachers. The small foul territory tended to put the fans right on top of the action. Gilmore was 335 feet down the foul lines and 400 feet to dead center. The intimacy of the park also gave fans a chance to check the movie stars who often attended. Former Twink first baseman Chuck Stevens notes

Gilmore Field, 1939

Gilmore Field and Stadium, c. 1939 (Courtesy, A.C. Gilmore Co.)

that casting directors also came to Gilmore. He played small parts in several movies, including the Warner Bros. epic, *Grover Cleveland Alexander*, starring former baseball broadcaster Ronald Reagan. Stevens' friend, Hall of Famer Bob Lemon, was Reagan's stand-in for the long shots of "Alexander" pitching. The postwar Stars were a powerhouse team. Under Fred Haney and Bobby Bragen they were league champs in 1949, 1952, and 1953. Their president, Bob Cobb, was instrumental in trying to build up the P.C.L. so it could eventually become a third major league. This met with scant interest from the American and National Leagues, of course. The stronger the rumors became of a bona fide major league team coming to Los Angeles, the less interest anyone had in gradually developing a new league.

The final straw came when CBS purchased the land under Gilmore Field and nearby Gilmore Stadium (used for football and midget car racing). The land was earmarked for the network's West Coast television headquarters. Notice was served to the Stars that their home field would be razed in 1958. Bob Cobb had hoped to move his team elsewhere in the Los Angeles area before it was announced that the Dodgers were definitely coming. He had been looking at land in the San Fernando Valley but was particularly attracted to a large parcel of land adjacent to downtown called Chavez Ravine.

THE DODGERS HEAD WEST

The Dodgers' move to the West Coast is basically a story of one city that was desperate to get a major league team and very aggressive in luring one, and another city that could never organize itself sufficiently to keep its two National League franchises.

Los Angeles had been in the market for a big league club since the St. Louis Browns' planned move west was interrupted by World War II. The city had plenty of empty land and was willing to use it as a bargaining chip. On the other coast, Walter O'Malley, principal stockholder of the Brooklyn Dodgers, had been telling New York officials for years that Ebbets Field no longer filled the bill. The Brooklyn ballpark and its manic fans occupy a favored place in the imagination of all baseball fans. But in point of fact, by the mid-1950s the park was in desperate need of repair, had almost no automobile parking, was served by only one subway line, found itself in a rapidly deteriorating neighborhood, and suffered from declining attendance. O'Malley wanted to build a new stadium at Atlantic and Flatbush Avenues in Brooklyn, which would have alleviated all of Ebbets Field's problems. This proposal was rejected. The best the city of New York would offer was the possibility of using some land in

Ebbets Field, c. 1944 (Courtesy, Los Angeles Dodgers)

Flushing Meadows in Queens. It wasn't as far away as Los Angeles, but this still would have taken the team out of Brooklyn.

While the Eastern city was delaying and telling O'Malley that none of his plans were feasible, Los Angeles, in the persons of Mayor Norris Poulson and his representatives, was doing everything in its power to lure the team to the other side of the continent. Land for a new stadium and millions of potential fans were the city's major chips.

Three other factors entered the equation. The 50-year-old homology of the major leagues ended in 1953 when the Braves left Boston for Milwaukee. The results were dramatic. Attendance rose from 281,278 in Boston to 1,826,397 in Milwaukee. Technology also played a role. Transcontinental jet passenger planes were just coming into service in 1957, making the long trip west feasible both in terms of time and cost. The third factor was that the Dodgers were not headed west alone. Their old crosstown rivals, the Giants, were coming along.

The Dodgers—which in the 1990 season will celebrate their centennial—officially announced the decision to move to Los Angeles on October 7, 1957. The major lure was the Chavez Ravine. The Dodgers wanted to build the stadium themselves, but they needed a city to condemn the land. It would take years of court cases before the transfer of the Ravine to the Dodgers would take place. The area had originally been a pleasant, semi-urban neighborhood of haphazardly arranged homes. All that was changed when it was renewed with a typical postwar vengeance starting in 1949. The old homes were flattened, the people moved out. A federally subsidized housing project called Elysian Park Heights was slated to rise on the site. This plan was condemned as creeping socialism in the Red Scare era of the early 1950s, and the city council voted to shelve the project in 1952. So when the city went looking for a place to offer the Dodgers as a ballpark site, Chavez Ravine was already largely vacant due to the abandoned plan for public housing.

While the courts were deciding just who had title to Chavez Ravine, the Dodgers set up shop in the Los Angeles Memorial Coliseum. This venerable stadium had been built in 1923 and was later expanded for the 1932 Olympics. In its time, it has hosted lots of football games, political and religious conventions, the celebration of the 150th anniversary of Los Angeles' cityhood, two Olympics, and several Bruce Springsteen concerts. But with its lack of shade in the summer heat and odd dimensions, it made a lousy baseball park.

Still, Dodger management was nothing if not creative. The only way to fit a baseball diamond in the Coliseum was to make the right field foul line a cozy 300 feet and the left-field line an absurd 251 feet. Center field zoomed out to 420 feet, with power alleys 375 to 400 feet from home plate. To compensate for

Ebbets Field, c. 1950 (Courtesy, Brooklyn Public Library)

the minuscule distance to left, a 42-foot-high screen was erected that ran 140 feet along the left-field fence. It was the same idea as Fenway Park in Boston – short field, tall wall. Only at the Coliseum people had to sit behind it, so the fence consisted of wire mesh. Sportswriters dubbed it the "Chinese screen." Dodger outfielder Wally Moon rearranged his left-handed swing and became famous for his "Moon shots" that were popped over the nearby wall. Pitchers referred to such blooper home runs as "screeno jobs."

The Dodger sojourn at the Coliseum lasted four years. While the team played baseball, management and city government were faced with a referendum on the transfer of ownership of Chavez Ravine to the Dodgers. The vote on June 3, 1958, was a narrow victory for the team. It would be another year and four months until a Supreme Court decision finalized the city's promises to the Dodgers as legal. Groundbreaking had taken place on September 17, 1959, while the appeal was still before the court. With the final hurdle cleared, the bulldozers gathered in earnest. It would take two and one half years and the movement of eight million cubic yards of earth to recontour the washes and gullies of Chavez Ravine into the ballpark envisioned by Walter O'Malley and his architect, Emil Praeger.

The official transfer of land involved trading the Chavez Ravine land for the Wrigley Field property. The city built the roads into the new park, but the Dodgers built the stadium itself with their own money. This used to be the common method of building a team's home field, but today Dodger Stadium is the only privately owned park in the major leagues.

Certainly the resulting ballpark was worth the wait. Dodger Stadium was been a hit with fans ever since the first game was played against the Cincinnati Reds on April 10, 1962. The seats are comfortable, the sight lines unobstructed, the feeling intimate and spacious at the same time. The place was pretty bare in 1962 but the trees and shrubs have slowly grown to create a parklike atmosphere as you approach the stadium from the acres of parking lots.

Sitting in the Top Deck General Admission seats, you can look out beyond the pavilion seats to the rolling hills of Southern California. Turning around, you get the best view of downtown Los Angeles available anywhere in the city. Dodger Stadium affords the fan not only a wonderful place to see a baseball game, but also the perfect representation of the nature of our national pastime – the sublime combination of America's rural past with its urban present.

Los Angeles' overwhelming desire to be a major league city was instrumental in bringing the Dodgers to Los Angeles. For the team, the main lures for venturing across the continent were all those fans and the chance to build the

L.A. Coliseum, 1959

perfect ballpark. Dodger Stadium is now the third oldest park in the National League. But with the meticulous care showered on it, the stadium should go on playing host to fans for decades to come.

THE DODGERS' CENTURY

The Dodgers' success in Los Angeles is the result of the happy merger of an indigenous minor league baseball tradition with a very old, well-organized major league club. The first Brooklyn National League team took the field in 1890. It was at first called the "Bridegrooms," because six of the players had recently married. The team soon became known as the Dodgers—shortened from Trolley Dodgers—in recognition of the constant challenge to team members in faithfully crossing the numerous streetcar lines in the growing borough of Brooklyn.

In its earliest days, the team played in Brooklyn's Washington Park, between 4th and 5th Avenues, at the foot of the neighborhood known as Park Slope. But the first real forerunner to L.A.'s Dodger Stadium opened in 1913 in a heavily Italian-American neighborhood known as Pigtown, east of Prospect Park. It was named for team president Charles Ebbets. Ebbets Field was the scene of lots of frustration during the 1920s and '30s—the Dodgers were constantly second-division—but the fans' patience was finally rewarded by the championship clubs of the late 1940s and '50s as well as by their chance to boo the hated Yankees as the two major league teams met in the "Subway World Series" of 1947, 1949, 1952, 1953, 1955, and 1956.

The Los Angeles Dodgers have always celebrated the team's long history, and have planned several centennial celebrations for the 1990 season. Among these are a series of baseball cards picturing every man who wore a Dodger uniform, exhibitions of art created by Los Angeles County schoolchildren depicting the team's history, and an Old Timers' Day game featuring players from among the 21 Brooklyn and Los Angeles National League pennant winners.

Baseball honors its past far more than the other professional sports. And the Dodgers have a longer and brighter history than most franchises. As the current players work to add to the story, 1990's fans will have the opportunity to cheer on both the team on the field and a century of predecessors!

Stan Williams, Don Drysdale, Danny McDevitt, Sandy Koufax,
Coliseum, 1959 (Photo Courtesy, Los Angeles Dodgers)

PART ONE: PRE-GAME

It is noon on a game day at Dodger Stadium. The coaches won't start arriving for another two and a half hours, the players for another three. The press box is empty. Its denizens won't be here until 5:00 or so. The gates won't be open to the fans for an hour after that. It is seven and a half hours until game time. At noon the stadium is largely empty. But not completely.

The Dodger offices scattered throughout the park are busy planning everything from future group visits to how many hot dogs to order for the next homestand, or possible trades to strengthen the team. Up on the Club Level, a maintenance man is repairing one of the seats. On the field the grounds keepers are at work sculpting the playing field. Outside the stadium, gardeners are seeing to the shrubbery that surrounds the ballpark. Somewhere else in the complex a video technician is checking his equipment, making certain it will be ready for the night's game.

The pace picks up considerably when the team gets ready for batting practice. This is the best time to be at the ballpark. One day, Tommy Lasorda is pitching a nine-inning "game" to a group of rookies just up from the minors. On another, Mike Scioscia and Fernando Valenzuela are playing home run derby. Everyday, starting and relieving pitchers will face each other in a hitting game umpired by coach Mark Cresse.

It is also a time of constant repetition. Hitters hustle in and out of the batting cage. Some call for a specific pitch, some just want to keep their swing sharp. Coaches are banging groundballs to the infielders. Another coach is popping fungoes to the outfielders. Kirk Gibson has a round of stretching exercises he does before every game. Other players are running in the outfield. It seems such chaos, but the pattern of pregame tuning up does not vary much. A quick infield practice will follow the visiting team's batting practice. After this, the Dodgers will go back to their dressing room through their dugout. They will change into fresh game uniforms and be ready for their night's work.

7:30 on a Los Angeles summer night. The stands are rapidly filling. The four umpires are walking to their positions. The ball boys are in position down the two foul lines. The players are milling in the dugout. Tonight's game will soon begin.

Mickey Hatcher, signing autographs, 1988

LASORDA'S GAME

It's not quite 4:00. The Dodgers wanting extra hitting are still in the clubhouse. They won't be in the batting cage for another fifteen minutes. Tommy Lasorda is on the mound at Dodger Stadium. Sixty-two years old. White hair. Very bowlegged. He's pitching against several prospects in their early twenties who have been called up from the Dodger minor league system for a year-end look. Gilberto Reyes, Chris Gwynn, and Mike Devereaux have just arrived. Tracy Woodson has spent much of the season with the team. These guys weren't even born when Lasorda last pitched for the Pacific Coast League Los Angeles Angels. Sixty-two or not, heat or not, Lasorda isn't giving the prospects an inch. He's throwing hard, mixing his pitches, brushing back hitters. He wants to win.

The rules of the game are simple. Lasorda gets five runs to start with and the hitters get nine innings to try and beat him. There is always an umpire from among the more experienced Dodger players. Today it is Rick Dempsey. It is up to the umpire to decide if the pitch is a ball or a strike, and if a batter connects, whether it is a hit or an out. If it's a hit, he has to say whether it is a single, double, or triple. These are major league ballplayers, so it is always decided before the pitch how deep the outfielders are playing, if they are shading the hitter, and so on.

Most of the decisions call for value judgments. Particularly as to what balls would be caught by infielders. If you think Tommy Lasorda would just good-naturedly put up with Dempsey ruling a groundball through the left side of the infield a base hit simply because he is the umpire, you don't know your man. The pitcher not only bitterly contests every throw he feels was miscalled – basically anything that is ruled a ball that didn't bounce in front of home plate first – but he rants, raves, and paws the dirt over a hit. When Dempsey ruled one of the hits to be a double, Lasorda registered his contrary opinion most vocally and at great length. After speaking his piece, he simply climbed back up the mound and brushed back the next hitter.

Several of the visiting Braves are sitting in the visitors' dugout watching the game. "Hey, Tommy," Dempsey calls out, "did you ever pitch against that guy Bobby Wine?" He is referring to the former infielder, now a Braves coach. "You bet I did," the pitcher yells. "And I loved it, too. Used to send a cab to his hotel just to make sure he showed up at the game. Oh, I had his number, all right." In the dugout, Wine laughs.

At that moment, Gilberto Reyes, one of the best prospects in the Dodger minor league system, strikes out. Dempsey first played in the major leagues in 1969. He understands the game and the people who play it. He is credited

Tommy Lasorda, pitching, 1988

with spotting a flaw in Tim Leary's delivery that helped the pitcher to have the best season of his career. "Hey, Tommy," he yells, "didn't you strike out some other guy once, Musical or something like that? Left-handed hitter, I think?"

"Yes, I did," says Lasorda professorially, leaning on the pitcher's protective screen. "A young man from Donora, Pennsylvania. Musial was his name. Went on to have a pretty good career, too. I'll tell you who else I struck out. That guy used to play outfield for the Giants. Mays was his name. I struck both those guys out, so don't you feel bad, young man. Those were two of the greatest hitters ever to play this game." Two batters later, Dempsey calls a line drive to left a single. "No, no, no!" Lasorda yells. "How could my man have missed that ball?!?" And the arguments start all over again.

After the day's game against the Braves, in the relative quite of the manager's office, I asked Lasorda what all the yelling and questioning of calls was really about. He explained that it was part of his job. "Any manager who's naive enough to think he's the one winning the games is in big trouble. All he can do is motivate and prepare both himself and his players. I want my players to know how important I think winning is. It's an attitude you have to instill in everything you do. Whether I'm pitching, managing, or playing cards – I want to win and I want my players to feel the same way."

Lasorda also notes that his pitching performances help him to get closer to new members of the team. "I love to be close to my players. I want them all to have fun here. I don't say this is the best or only way to manage, but it's my way and it works for me."

Major league baseball is a business. It's hard to get a job and just as hard to keep one once you've got it. Never is it merely a game. Certainly not the nightly nine innings, and not even the pre-game duel between the pitcher/manager and four players new to the team. Desire, discipline, talent. Skills constantly honed. Desire constantly stoked. It's the only way to get to the big leagues and the only way to stay there. Lasorda had not been just tossing some batting practice today. He had been passing on his burning desire to win.

Tommy Lasorda, exhorting, 1988

THE PITCHER'S GAME

As every baseball purist knows, the American League's designated hitter rule is an abomination, a direct challenge to the wrath of Mother Nature. The National League may dominate in the use of the equally loathsome plastic grass, but at least its pitches still take their turn at the plate as God intended.

Certainly no one takes their hitting any more seriously than the hurlers themselves. Their turn in the batting cage comes after players who feel they need extra hitting have taken their cuts. Prior to this, several of the pitchers have been bunting a baseball back and forth, trying to keep it in the air. With their batting eye thus fortified, they are ready to face Todd Maulding, Tom Aloi, or one of the other batting-practice pitchers.

They play a game similar to Tommy Lasorda's. The only difference is that the two teams are starters vs. relievers. Bullpen coach Mark Cresse is the umpire. He decides whether the batter deserves a hit or an out. He gets only slightly less respect from his pitchers than Rick Dempsey did from Lasorda. These are professional athletes. Desire, talent, and aggression are what got them this far. They do not take failure, even in a meaningless batting-practice game, with magnanimity.

Orel Hershiser will start today, so he will hit later on with the other players in the opening lineup. The pitcher was standing next to the batting cage cheering on his mates when I approached to ask how the game worked. In his serious, soon-to-become-president-of-the-bank manner, Hershiser explained about the umpire and what was a hit, what an out. Just as he was mentioning how seriously all the pitchers took this game, Danny Heep walked by. "Sure, they take it seriously," he says. "There's a thousand dollars riding on each game." Hershiser smiles. "Well, that's a colorful story and you can print it if you want, but the truth is that this is just for bragging rights when we're out shagging balls. And we do brag." On another day, during the pitcher's batting practice, I happened to be back in the clubhouse. Don Sutton was tossing a baseball against the concrete wall, playing catch with himself. When asked why he wasn't out hitting, he replied, "I'm too lousy, they won't let me play." Brian Holton walked by and saw Sutton. Apparently it had been a rough game. "Jeez, the hits were so scarce today we could've even used you." Sutton continues tossing the ball against the wall. "Pitchers shouldn't have to hit anyway. If the other eight guys can't produce, we deserve to lose."

Pitchers prepare for their game, 1988

BATTING-PRACTICE PITCHER

When you arrive at the stadium four hours before the game, the field is virtually empty. A few players are getting in some extra batting practice before the pitchers enter the cage. Dodger coach Joe Ferguson is pitching. Before the visiting team comes out to the cage, coaches Bill Russell and Mark Cresse will also pitch. So will Juarez Orman, Tom Aloi, Harry McMillian, and Todd Maulding. These latter are batting-practice pitchers. Their job is to get the ball over the plate for the hitters. It may not be center stage, but it is a part of the show.

This afternoon, Juarez Orman is throwing to the pitchers. They are playing their usual starters versus relievers game, with Mark Cresse umpiring. Orman has been doing this a long time and takes pride in what he does. There will be few pitches outside the strike zone.

No one starts out as a batting-practice pitcher. Bill Russell was a shortstop, Joe Ferguson a catcher. Juarez Orman began his career with the Dodgers selling souvenirs in 1967. At the end of that season, he asked outfielder Lou Johnson whether there was any way he could get a job on the field. A few days later he was in a Dodger uniform as the right-field ball boy. It was a good life, but the next year he found himself in the Army.

Lying on a cot in Da Nang and Chu Lai, South Vietnam, Orman's thoughts often turned back to the stadium. He played catch to stay in shape when possible. He returned to part-time work with the Dodgers after getting out of the service. In 1973, he was given a golden opportunity. The Dodgers gave him a tryout. He was put on the mound and told to see what he could do with Steve Garvey. As it turned out, he could do little. Garvey hit his fast ball, his curve and his change up. But he at least had his chance.

Three years later, Orman was back at the stadium as a batting-practice pitcher. In the past fifteen years, he has missed only eight games. He works full-time for the city of Los Angeles now, but for 81 games a year he pitches at Dodger Stadium. It is harder to stay in shape at thirty-nine than at twenty-nine, but he has adjusted. His ball has considerable movement on it, which is popular with some of the players (Mike Scioscia and Mike Marshall, in particular), and he does his job well. It is not without its cost. During the off season, Orman plays on a Sunday League team. All year he will run and do push ups and lift weights. He has to keep his shoulder and elbow strong. Why go through all this for a part-time job? "Well," he notes of his time on the mound, "it is a lotta fun."

Juarez Orman pitching, 1989

THE HITTING COACH

The manager is responsible for the overall performance of his team. He is assisted in the pennant chase by a legion of specialists on his coaching staff. With the Dodgers, Bill Russell coaches the infielders, Ron Perranoski the pitchers, Mark Cresse is in charge of the bullpen, Joe Amalfitano relays signals at third base and studies opposing fielders, and Ben Hines and Manny Mota counsel the hitters. All of them are in evidence during pre-game workouts.

While the coaches are going about their various tasks, Mike Davis is taking his cuts in the batting cage. This has been a tough year for the former Oakland Athletic. He was scheduled to add a long-ball punch to the Dodger lineup when he started in right field in April. By mid-season Mike Marshall had left first base and returned to the outfield. Mike Davis became a role player. Where did his stroke go? He was in the batting cage before every game, trying to find that out.

One of the duties of the batting instructor is to help hitters find out the cause of a slump. Manny Mota is one of the Dodger hitting coaches. As an active player he collected a major league record 150 pinch hits, so he knows a little something about hitting a baseball. His pre-game post is directly behind the batting cage, watching the players take their cuts. Mota notes that he spends so much time behind the cage because players "prepare themselves for the game right here in batting practice." His attention is always on a hitter's mechanics. How does the batter approach the ball? Where are his hands and head? How is he shifting his body as the ball approaches? Has he changed his swing? Things done a thousand times. But the slightest unconscious change can disrupt the entire flow and lead to a slump. It is the coach's job to make sure this does not happen.

Manny Mota will also watch videos of the game to look for the telltale glitch in a man's swing. But he prefers to study from the back of the cage, because, "if we correct a problem here, it will never get into the game."

So, there he is, every day. Standing on the rollers of the batting cage. Watching. He might periodically shout out some advice or encouragement, but mostly he is there to observe.

Hitting coach Manny Mota, 1988

MISSISSIPPI MUD FROM
THE DELAWARE RIVER

Baseball is full of arcane practices linked to the dim recesses of its 19th-century roots. With four and a half hours remaining prior to game time, Walt Atamanuck is buried deep in the bowels of Dodger Stadium engaged in one of them. His official title is Umpire's Attendant. But his first duty at every home game is to rub up seven dozen baseballs. The official name of the glop rubbed on the shiny new balls is Lena Blackburne Baseball Rubbing Mud. It is known throughout organized baseball as Mississippi Mud in spite of the fact that it is gathered from some secret spot of the bed of the Delaware River in New Jersey. Each team in the majors and minors is sent a one-pound jar of the stuff at the beginning of the season. Walt's counterparts throughout baseball will use the compound to take the slippery sheen off the ball, thereby allowing the pitcher to get a better grip on it.

Sitting on a chair in the umpire's room, Walt prepares to rub up the baseballs for tonight's game. He transfers the mud from the large Blackburne jar to a small cat food can. This makes the stuff easier to use. He gets his right hand damp with water, and gets a little mud on his left hand. He rubs the mixture over the ball, being careful to not get it too dark, which irritates the hitters, or mud in the seams, which is a problem to the pitchers. The freshly rubbed balls are tossed into a ball can that will be placed in the Dodger dugout along with the four dozen previously prepared balls kept on hand in case of emergency. The home plate umpire will keep a maximum of six balls in a pouch. When he runs out, he signals to the Dodger bat boy to bring him some more.

Walt watches the early part of the game from the stands. In the fifth inning he will start to prepare the umpire's room. After the game they will have dinner provided by the home team. Walt's wife, Jan, sometimes bakes the umpiring crew a cake, or makes a few sandwiches and a fruit tray for a pre-game snack. She often sends a flower arrangement in with her husband just to cheer up the concrete-block room. Walt has hung some landscape paintings on the walls for the same reason. A VCR is also in the room. After the game, the umpires may request a copy of the video tape shot by the Dodgers to review a controversial play among themselves behind closed doors.

Walt retired from the U.S. Post Office in 1980 and started working with the Dodgers. He has been rubbing up baseballs for the past three seasons, and considers it his best job with the team yet. "Hey, how else would I have gotten into the Hall of Fame?" Well, some of his baseballs, anyway. The ball from the first game of the 1988 World Series may have moved into the hall because of the historic import of the moment, but it started its day in Walt's hands.

Walt Atamanuck rubbing in the Mississippi Mud, 1989

DANNY HEEP

It's 4:45 and the pitchers are through hitting. Today the relievers won. Close game, though. Next to hit are the non-starters. Danny Heep, one of the most intense men on the Dodgers, is part of this group. The desire and hunger to succeed are palpable when speaking to him. He is one of the Stuntmen, the bench strength the Dodgers have relied on all season. But there isn't a non-pitcher in the major leagues who doesn't want to play every day. Heep is no exception.

I asked Steve Sax if the major leagues had been like he expected. Even better, the starting second baseman said. Not so for Heep. He stresses how hard he has to work to stay on the roster. Every spring when he reports, he feels he has to win a place on the team all over again. He translates the stress from the situation into desire. He never reports out of shape. The official training period may begin in March, but Heep has been working out with friends and other ballplayers ever since December near his home in San Antonio, Texas. He has never been someone who could coast on his native ability. Heep has always had to train longer and harder than the player with lots of raw talent in order to stay in the big leagues.

What does a man with this much intensity do when he sits down so much? How does he cope with the horror of his June 6th start at unfamiliar first base when he made two errors, and the crowd sarcastically cheered him when he made a routine play? On that occasion, Heep turned to the first-base-side crowd and doffed his cap. Normally, he just has to keep it to himself because he is a role player, not a starter. He has to practice and stay sharp, constantly honing his ability in order to stay in the big leagues. It is very frustrating, but as Heep points out, "What I can never do," Heep points out, "is take the frustration home. That could ruin my family. The game has to stay at the ballpark."

Today, Danny Heep is not starting. He will hit with the other Stuntmen. Then he will shag balls and run in the outfield. Once the game starts, he will watch from the dugout and try to stay mentally alert. He is a role player and tonight if he is going to contribute to his team, the role will be to pinch-hit. So he watches the opposing team's pitcher, takes a few cuts at the pitching machine under the stands, and stays ready. All the while the intensity burns.

Danny Heep, 1988

BILLY BEAN

Colleges function as a free minor league system for professional basketball and football. This has traditionally not been the case with baseball. A few college men, like Christy Mathewson and Charlie Gehringer, spotlight the history of baseball. But the ballplayer of legend, as described in Bernard Malamud's novella *The Natural*, springs from his youth with talent fullblown. Bullet Bob Feller walked in off the farm in Van Meter, Iowa. Babe Ruth was rescued from the streets of Baltimore by Brother Mathias. Joe DiMaggio moved from sandlot ball in San Francisco to the Pacific Coast League and the Yankees. Frank Merriwell is one of the only popular culture sports heroes to take seriously his education. Americans as a people have never been as interested in learning as they have been in the higher salary that generally attends a university degree.

In spite of baseball myths of the past, more ballplayers are getting a higher education before they start their professional careers. Reggie Jackson came to the A's out of Arizona State. Roger Clemens pitched in the College World Series for the University of Texas before winning the Cy Young Award with the Red Sox. One of the newest of the 1989 Dodgers is also a college player.

Billy Bean grew up in Santa Ana and played ball at Loyola–Marymount University in Los Angeles. Since he was born in Orange County, some 30 miles south of Dodger Stadium, he saw mostly Angel games as a kid. Coming to the Dodgers out of the Tigers organization has been great for Bean. "It's always been a dream to play in my hometown." Their minor league system is also more oriented to teaching than had been the case with Detroit's. When he reported to Albuquerque, the Dodger AAA team, he found to his delight that there were two more full-time coaches than had been the case with his previous team in Louisville.

Bean noted several differences between baseball in college and the minor leagues. The main one is the fewer games in college and the constant emphasis on its being a team sport. In the minors, you played everyday, but the team is secondary. Everyone wants this to be as momentary a stopover as possible. Baseball in the minors is a job, and the job is to get out of town and into the majors. All the players are aware of the constant reports going from their managers and the owner's scouts to the major league team that owns their contract. It is individual play that is the subject of those conversations, not how the team is doing.

Baseball life has been a series of mental adjustments for Billy Bean. Managers, coaches, front office personnel – and the player himself – all have expectations as a man works his way through baseball's complex hierarchy. The outfielder notes, "I don't think you can anticipate the pressure and anxiety of everyday major league ball." You focus so much on the details of your game. The competition is more stringent. Outside distractions get worse. But this is the life Bean chooses for himself, and he is determined to succeed at it.

Billy Bean and Mickey Hatcher, 1989

BILL RUSSELL

Bill Russell's uniform is in the Hall of Fame at Cooperstown, New York, along with those of Steve Garvey, Davey Lopes, and Ron Cey. They were together as an infield unit from 1973 to 1981, longer than any other infield in major league history. Garvey eventually went to the Padres, Lopes to the Astros, and Cey to the Cubs. Russell never left. He retired as a player in 1986 and joined the coaching staff the following year. After beginning his career as a center fielder, Russell was turned into a shortstop. All the dedication and work it took to learn a new position stands him in good stead as he instructs the current crop of Dodger infielders.

Russell will arrive at the stadium about 3:00 for a night game. The stands are empty. The batting cage is in place, but not yet in use. The coaches are just arriving. Some of the players are parking their cars in their lot behind the home bullpen. Bill Russell is in the outfield, in shorts and a University of Oklahoma tee-shirt, running. None of the fire that drove him through 17 seasons of major league baseball has been banked. He is still too close to his playing days to easily accept their being completely over. But he knows they are. So Bill Russell is working hard at becoming as good a coach as possible.

Batting practice is pitched by the coaches or other non-rooster players. Mark Cresse, Joe Ferguson, and Bill Russell will all pitch to the Dodgers. Their main job is to deliver consistently hittable balls to the Dodger hitters. As soon as Russell has completed his stint on the mound, he will start hitting groundballs to the infielders.

Once the game starts the coaches can only advise. They watch their players and make notes about their performance. If Tommy Lasorda has a question, they'd better have an answer. Certainly every coach wants to do his job. It is a challenge, and it is a way to stay a part of the game they have loved their entire lives. But what if you want to do more than watch, teach, and advise? What if in your heart you know you can still play – no matter what numbers you may have put up in your last year as an active player?

What you do is your new job. The talents slide long before the tiger that leads a man to the major leagues dies.

Bill Russell, 1988

THE CATCHER AND THE ACTOR

The pre-game field is full of visitors. Two of them on this day are doing research for an upcoming movie called *Major League*. Steve Yeager was the starting catcher for the Dodger teams of the 1970s and early '80s. He shared the World Series Most Valuable Player award with Pedro Guerrero and Ron Cey in 1981. After playing with the Dodgers for three more seasons, Yeager wound up his career in Seattle. He does very well leasing cars now, but his previous line of work helped land him a part-time job as the technical adviser for the proposed movie. Tom Berrenger was nominated for a best supporting Oscar for his work in *Platoon* in 1987. He has played soldiers, ex-rock and roll singers, and lots of other parts. Now he is slated to be a catcher.

Hollywood and baseball go back a long way. Until the success of *The Natural* in 1984, baseball movies were usually seen as less than sure things at the box office. Boxing movies have the luxury of being able to concentrate on the physical and moral dilemmas of only one man. It's more complicated when you have to deal with an entire team. But in Los Angeles, the Pacific Coast League Hollywood Stars pioneered in uniting the team and the film industry. Not only did several performers own part interest in the club, the Stars were also the first to establish the continually popular exhibition game between various film and television celebrities and a team from the press.

Yeager's job on the film is to make the ballplaying in it look authentic. But now he is back home. Today at the park he talks to old friends, introduces Berrenger to some of the players, and answers questions from a reporter who is curious about what he might be thinking about. It turns out that, among other things, his thoughts have turned to one more try. He hated that last season with the Mariners in a city crazy for football but uninterested in their second-division baseball team. He wonders aloud about one more try. Could he still play?

You listen and marvel at the engine that drives the professional athlete. Yeager isn't talking about money or fame. He's talking about wanting to still be a part of a game he played so well that he was welcomed into the company of its most select practitioners. He wonders if he still can.

Steve Yeager and Tom Berrenger, 1988

"MR. CUB" IN DODGER BLUE

You never know what you might stumble over around the batting cage before a game. This is Los Angeles, after all, so it was no particular surprise to see an actor standing around studying for an upcoming role. But I was taken aback to see Ernie Banks taking some cuts one afternoon. It was no shock to see the Hall of Fame shortstop batting, but "Mr. Cub" was wearing a Dodger uniform! When asked about this, Banks replied, "I had no choice. Tommy wouldn't let me wear a Cubs uniform out here."

As it happens, Ernie Banks was not out at the stadium getting in a few cuts just for the sake of conditioning. He was on his way to England to meet cricket champion Graham Gooch in a home run derby. Since he now lives in the Los Angeles area, Banks asked Tommy Lasorda if he could come out to Dodger Stadium and take a few cuts with his son, Joey, before heading overseas. So here he was in a Dodger uniform, snapping those wonderful wrists at batting-practice pitching.

Joey Banks played infield for U.S.C. The day at Dodger Stadium gave him a rare chance to play ball with his father, who is now a vice president with the Andrex Corporation. Ernie serves as a liaison between the real estate development company and the international business community. He has also held executive positions with the Cubs, Equitable Life Insurance, Associated Films Promotion, and New World Van Lines. But it was neither the business success nor the challenges of Graham Gooch that made the players smile in recognition and come over to shake hands. They wanted to meet the ballplayer whose talent led him to Cooperstown having become one of only 14 men to hit over 500 home runs.

I was not the only reporter to notice Banks. A film crew from KABC was asking people to explain the concept of the "magic number" – that mixture of victories and other teams' defeats that guarantees a pennant. If the TV crew expected to get a tongue-tied ex-ballplayer, they were disappointed. What they get was a vice president who delivered a quick, lucid, right-to-the-point answer to their question.

Joey and Ernie Banks, 1988

GORDON VERRELL

Batting practice is almost over. Gordon Verrell of the *Long Beach Press Telegram* is interviewing shortstop Dave Anderson. One of the "Stuntmen," Anderson has done an excellent job replacing Alfredo Griffin, whose right hand was fractured by a Dwight Gooden fastball. As Verrell asks his questions, Anderson stretches, loosening his muscles for the day's game.

Verrell has been at the stadium since 5:00. He and the representatives of seven other Southland newspapers spend their pre-game time asking questions and observing. Before the advent of television and radio broadcasts of all games, much of a sportswriter's story of the day's game was taken up with a description of the action. Today's scribe is constantly in need of a hook, an inside story. Most fans either heard the game on the radio, or saw a synopsis of it on the nighttime news. When they pick up a newspaper, they're looking for more than who got the game-winning hit. So Verrell and his comrades are out early, watching and questioning.

The information gleaned from a pre-game interview will often be sent to the newspaper during the game as a "starter" for the day's story. The sound of a typewriter is now vaguely annoying in the press room. All the beat reporters use laptop computers and phone in stories directly to their office. The voice of the official scorer is easily heard over the light clicking of dozens of reporters processing words. The *Press Telegram*'s deadline is usually about 10:45. But baseball is a notorious non-respecter of the clock. If the game runs long, Verrell sends in a "running" story. An editor receives the story, revises it to his liking, makes up a headline, and sends the finished story off to composing.

Verrell notes that writers are "an extension of the fan." He feels responsible for explaining the game and gauging the mood of the team for his readers. He wants to get at the truth of the situation but feels it is important to remember you're dealing with a real person. "We just can't come barging in there. You've gotta respect their feelings."

But you've also got to find the truth. It's this sparring and the daily challenge of a new game that is the key to baseball's attraction for Gordon Verrell. He covers a variety of sports, but always looks forward to spring and the start of a new season.

Dave Anderson and Gordon Verrell, 1988

LENNY HARRIS AND FRIENDS

Pitching was the key highlight of the 1989 season for the Dodgers. Their 2.95 staff E.R.A. led the major leagues. They allowed the fewest runs, and hurled the most shutouts. But the hitting never seemed to jell, with the timely hit being particularly elusive. But no one was running away with the National League West. So, in July, the team traded to try and strengthen their meager offense. Pitcher Tim Leary and infielder Mariano Duncan were sent to Cincinnati for Kal Daniels and Lenny Harris. Time will tell how successful the trade was in terms of the Dodgers' standing in their division, but they were able to secure one of the premier gadabouts in major league baseball with the acquisition of Lenny Harris.

I first saw Harris in action when the Dodgers were playing his old team, the Reds. Fraternization between teams is officially frowned on by the league, but it is common to see members of different teams talking by the batting cage before the game. The Dodgers were still hitting when the Reds came out of the visitors' clubhouse and started doing aerobic exercises on the grass near the batting cage. As would be the case with the Giants when they came to town, the younger players enthusiastically joined in the stretching and twisting, while the older players only went through the motions. But the Dodgers certainly did not pass up a chance to make fun of the Reds. Mickey Hatcher watched all this and yelled at them, "Where's the music?" When Ken Griffey saw Eddie Murray watching, he yelled over to him, "Watch this one, Eddie." On the call from the aerobics leader, the younger players set about enthusiastically pretzeling themselves. Griffey and Murray looked on bemusedly.

Once the exercises were over, Harris started talking with Griffey and Herm Winningham. Tim Leary and Mariano Duncan had been speaking with friends on the Dodgers, so it seemed natural that Harris would follow suit. But every time I saw him before a game he was talking to someone else. This is just the man's character. He is naturally gregarious and has several good friends from around the league whom he always looks forward to spending time with.

But the laughs before a game, and the comfortable meal after a game with an opposing player, are one thing. When the game starts, "we got no respect for each other." Harris is a professional ballplayer. He wants to play for a long time to come. He is in the process of challenging other Dodgers for a position on the starting team. For nine innings, there are only teammates and opponents.

Ken Griffey, Lenny Harris (center), and Herm Winningham, 1989

THE NATIONAL TREASURE

One of the oldest truisms in baseball is that the best managers come from the ranks of journeymen players. For many, this is true. Walt Alston had a grand total of one major league at bat. Tommy Lasorda pitched in 26 games in the majors with an 0 and 4 record. Hall of Famers may manage, but they rarely add much to the glory of their playing days. But here, as in so many other ways, Yogi Berra is an exception.

The three-time Most Valuable Player is only one of five managers in the history of baseball to take teams to the World Series in both leagues. For the past four seasons, he has been a coach with the Houston Astros. This came about due to his friendship with team chairman John McMullen, who happens to live in Berra's neighborhood. Berra has been in a baseball uniform ever since returning from sea duty in World War II. 1989 will be his last season as a coach. It seems somehow unnatural to not have Yogi Berra on a baseball field.

Like most coaches, you will find Yogi leaning against the batting cage before a game. A constant stream of both Dodgers and Astros come up to him. Willie Randolph, new to the Dodgers in 1989 after thirteen seasons with the Yankees, came over to say hello to his former manager. Ben Hines, the Dodger hitting coach, traded quips with him. Tommy Lasorda told him Italian jokes. But Berra is a coach. When the time comes, Berra, like everyone else in uniform around the batting cage, goes out and picks up the loose balls lying around. He may be a legend and focus of attention, but he also has a job to do.

To Berra, Los Angeles is just another stop on the road. He has no favorite place to eat out here, no particular place to hang out. He does like Dodger Stadium. The field is in good shape, the crowds are big, and, he says, "This is nice because they keep it so clean." He also has fond memories of old Wrigley Field. Berra's only chance to play there was in the Angels' inaugural season in the American League. A true hitter, he fondly remembers that "the ball went outa there pretty good."

Soon he was talking to Kevin Bass about hitting, holding an imaginary bat and making a point about stepping toward the pitch. Here was Yogi Berra in his element, passing on the knowledge gained from over 40 years in the game. He is a man who coined some of the most commonly heard catch phrases in America, including his most famous observation, "It ain't over 'til it's over." He's probably the only baseball player to have a cartoon character named after him. An American institution.

When batting practice ended, he went out to the pitcher's mound, picking up baseballs along the way.

Yogi Berra and Bill Doran, 1989

THE FOOD STAND

Annette Soldano runs one of the premier food stands at the stadium. It is on the lower level where the seats are the most expensive. Annette and her sixteen co-workers are employed by the Arthur Foods Co., the food concessionaire for Dodger Stadium. It is a little past 5:00. Annette and her crew have been here for fifteen minutes already. Peanuts, popcorn, and candy bars are being taken out of their storage boxes and placed on the shelves. The stand won't open to customers for another hour. A few early fans drift in by 6:30. By 7:00 the lines are stretching the length of the booth. Business is generally steady all night until the beer is shut off in the bottom of the seventh inning. The stand will close soon after the end of the game, but the crew doesn't leave until everything has been cleaned and the remaining food stored away.

Two of the workers will be particularly busy tonight. Before she turns off the spigot after the seventh inning, Gina Musacco will pour over 600 glasses of beer. Her official title at the stand is bartender, but she knows nothing about mixing drinks. She only pours beer. Working on the nearby grill, David Taliaferro will prepare over 1,400 hot dogs for hungry fans. And this is only one stand.

Like most of the other people working at Dodger Stadium, Annette has the best of both worlds. She likes her job and the extra money it brings her, and she loves baseball. David is the same. He confesses to being a "baseball fanatic." He drives for U.P.S. all year, but plans to continue cooking for the 81 home games "as long as I can work it around my other job schedule." To someone who loves the game, work for Arthur Foods offers the ultimate fringe benefit. When you are all caught up with your work, you can walk a few paces and watch the Dodgers play.

Annette Saldano prepares her food stand, 1988

HAWKERS AND SCORECARDS

Matt Seymour is sitting on a fold-up chair outside the vendor storage area on the lower level. Inside, several young men are loading up their baskets with yearbooks, scorecards, pennants, Dodger dolls, and other souvenirs. Matt is a guard. He will be stationed here all night. This is his ninth season with the Dodgers. He misses seeing the game, but enjoys the extra pay he gets as a guard. When he was an usher he met lots of people and saw all the games. Now he only watches the vendors come and go and gives periodic directions. But he does get time to study. He finds that an excellent fringe benefit now that he's in college.

Inside the storage area, Furious Stroud and his cousin, Kevin Battle, are loading the last of the souvenirs in their baskets. They are known in the trade as hawkers, and will spend most of the game walking up and down the aisles trying to interest fans in taking home a souvenir. Both note that the load gets pretty heavy after a few innings, but say that the 20-percent commission they earn on their sales make the walking worth it. It's almost 6:00 and they will be heading off to the stands soon. They will return whatever they don't sell in the seventh inning. Both agree that bats, pennants, and programs sell the best.

It is now after 7:00. Fans are rushing to get in the gate and to their seats before the first pitch. In a prime location between the first-level seats and the Left Field Pavilion, Don Buschhoff is calling, "Hey, you've got to have a program here." He had been selling novelties at the Coliseum when the Dodgers arrived in 1958. He thinks it was a lousy place for baseball, with very few good seats for the fans. Business was always brisk, but he was very happy when the new stadium opened. The only thing he missed about the Coliseum was the Nighthawk restaurant on Vermont. "Had the best chili in town," he remembers. Don sells programs at sports venues all over Los Angeles, and notes that football fans are the most likely to buy a program because each one is different. Sales of baseball scorecard magazines can slow down drastically toward the end of the monthly cycle of the program. A poor showing in the standings by the home team late in the season also puts a damper on sales.

Furious Stroud prepares his hawkers' basket, 1988

TELEVISION CREWS

Baseball has never translated to television all that well. Too much of the action is individual. If the camera is covering the left fielder catching a fly ball, it can't be watching the runner tagging up at third base. The man scoring is important and always seems to be recorded. But often there is a throw to second or third to try and catch an advancing runner that is therefore missed. Football, on the other hand, is the ultimate television game. The action tends to be considerably more grouped and there are always cheerleaders around for the wandering camera to shamelessly ogle. It is no surprise that the onset of professional football's popularity was coincident with the spread of personal television ownership.

Radio is omnipresent at Dodger Stadium, but the TV crews are usually around only at the start of the game for a 6:00 news quick spot or at the end of the season if the team is fighting for first place. Other than that, local sports shows just use highlights from the feed provided by Video Tape Enterprises. But now it is late September and the Dodgers are fighting for a championship. Television crews are all over the place. A print reporter just stands there with his pad, talking and scribbling. The television personality rarely goes anywhere without a cameraman and soundman. It makes for a crowded pre-game foul territory this time of year. One of the video crews filming the late-season Dodgers belongs to Jim McDonald. He is the president of Saturday House, and is taping anti-smoking segments for the American Cancer Society. He has shot segments in various major league parks, but notes that the Dodgers have been the most helpful and professional of all the organizations .

McDonald is not entirely without prejudice on the subject of the Dodgers. He is from the East New York section of Brooklyn and spent as much of his youth as possible in Ebbets Field. He sees the difference in the new and old Dodgers as being "mainly the fans. There is nothing in this world like a Brooklyn baseball fan. Loyal, rabid, and vocal." As for the organization, he doesn't think it has changed at all. "They were a class act in Ebbets Field and they're a class act in Dodger Stadium."

Tommy Lasorda receives an award from René Cardenas, 1988

THE EMPTY SIDELINES

The Dodgers could hardly move around before their late-September games in 1988. They were ready to clinch the pennant and the media wanted to interview and photograph them. In 1989, it was a different story. There was no one around asking inane questions about the magic number and Orel Hershiser was not in the middle of setting the record for consecutive scoreless innings pitched. The '89 Dodgers were going to have to look forward to 1990.

There were still some video crews on the sidelines before the games. RayMar Productions was filming a video that concerned Christian ballplayers giving testimony as to their faith. John Shelby and Mike Davis both spoke, wearing a hat that displayed a Jesus symbol. Tim Teufel of the Mets also recorded a message. Ray Martinez explained that the video would be presented free of charge to whoever "wants to hear the message." He wanted to use athletes on the tape because he felt it was important to present the image of a strong Christian. "It's important that kids be shown that you aren't a wimp just because you have a relationship with Christ."

The Los Angeles Unified School District was out filming some segments for *Homework Hot Line*. Rebecca Hurst had Jay Howell reading a message urging kids to do their homework. She noted that students listened more to athletes than to actors. The idea of *Hot Line* is to give kids a place to call in when they have a question about school. The live show is presented on Channel 58 from October to June.

The photo wells were as underpopulated as the pre-game sidelines. The standard crew of the A.P., U.P.I., and the *Times* were still at work, but the visitors from *Sports Illustrated* and the networks were following the Giants and Cubs around. One of the few visitors was James Caras of Troy, New York. He and his wife, Jeanne, were in Los Angeles to celebrate his sister's 25th Jubilee as a nun in the Presentation Order. Sr. James Marie is both a lifelong resident of upstate New York and a Dodger fan. The Carases could not think of a better gift than a trip to Los Angeles to see her favorite baseball team. Through a series of long-distance phone calls and letters, James not only arranged for some nice seats at the stadium, but also for a photo of his sister with Tommy Lasorda. Caras is a photographer for a newspaper in Albany, New York, and spent the game in the photo well shooting his beloved Mets. His wife and sister were on the Loge Level, Sr. James Marie cheering on the Dodgers.

When the game ended, Jeanne came to the rail on the second level and shouted down to the photo well. She was wearing a Mets tee-shirt, waving and smiling at her husband. He looked up at her, waved back, smiled happily, and began folding up his tripod.

Tim Teufel and Ray Martinez, 1989

ALL THE ATTENTION

In September 1988, Orel Hershiser and Kirk Gibson could not go out on the field without someone stopping them for a question, photograph, or interview. The Dodgers were the obvious choice to win the National League West title and there was press everywhere. In 1989, Hershiser was merely a bright spot in a poor season and Gibson was on the disabled list. The Dodgers were out of the race and only the daily press were at the park. Until the Giants paid a visit.

Suddenly the sidelines were jammed before the game just like in 1988. Only the crews were set up near the visitors' dugout. This season the Giants had a lock on the pennant and the media was going to be there when they officially clinched. In 1989, it was Kevin Mitchell and Will Clark who could not leave the dugout without attracting a crowd.

Reporters do tend to ask the same questions over and over. In Mitchell's case, they all want to know about the rough San Diego neighborhood he grew up in. How did sports save him? How did his family help to keep him out of gangs? Then there are the home run questions. How many can he hit? Why so many more this year? What about the different pitchers around the League? Will the Giants win it all? And so on. All Kevin Mitchell wants to do is take batting practice. But there is a phalanx of media people, notebooks at the ready, cameramen in position, who are lined up waiting for him. It is not their fault that the questions are all the same. There is only so much you can ask a ballplayer. But if a news organization is to be taken seriously it must send its people to the major stories. Where 30 years ago players on the league's leading team had only to deal with the local papers and the wire services, now there is an army of news gatherers with orders to get a leading player on camera or in a quote.

Sports has come to be one of the predominant safety valves for the national psyche. So much of modern life is overwhelming in its implications. What does it mean that there is a hole in the ozone layer? What will be the global effect of the destruction of the Amazon rain forests? Crime is endemic in the United States. Death squads operate openly in Central America and Sri Lanka. Airliners are blown to bits in midair for political reasons. Horrifying sexually transmitted diseases have graduated from being merely incurable to being deadly. Drugs and homelessness plague every city in America.

Horror after horror. "Live at five" and in color. The nightly news has become such a tale of surreal perversity that news gatherers are desperate to alleviate the gloom. Sports helps. It is something harmless. Something with a winner and loser. Easy to tell the best from the worst. Simple. A lifeline in the chaos. So whoever takes Kevin Mitchell's place as the hot item of 1990 can expect to deal with more stacks to reporters, asking the same questions for all those fans who are so desperate for diversion and the grandeur of the winner.

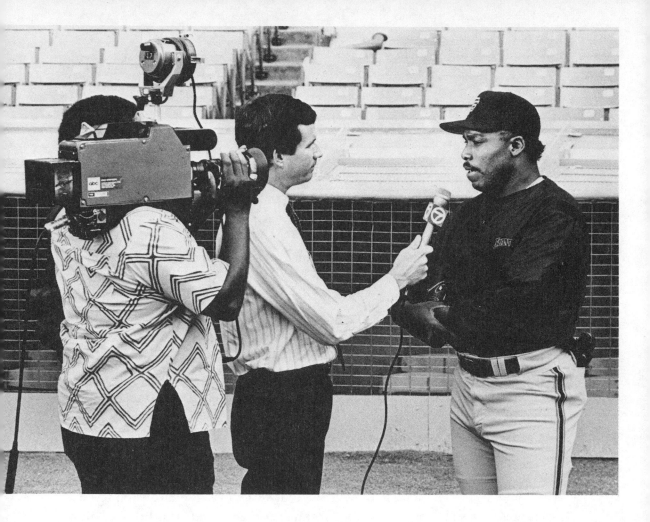

Kevin Mitchell with video men, 1989

DON DRYSDALE

Ever since the Dodgers came west from Brooklyn in 1958, Vin Scully and Jerry Doggett announced the games. The team was joined by Ross Porter in 1977 when Scully started doing more network sports. Doggett retired in 1987 and the question of his replacement had to be faced. The Dodgers were able to keep it in the family. Hall of Fame pitcher Don Drysdale, who along with Sandy Koufax was the heart and soul of the great Dodger teams of the mid-1960s, left his announcing job with the Chicago White Sox and ABC-TV to return to Los Angeles.

It is about 45 minutes before game time and Drysdale is standing outside the press dining room, sipping some soda pop. In response to a question about how it feels to be back at Dodger Stadium, he looks out over the field covered with Astros taking batting practice, and says, "Well, it's like coming back home." Double so for Drysdale, who grew up in Van Nuys. Tickets and transportation to Wrigley Field to see the Pacific Coast League Angels was a luxury not always affordable in the Drysdale home. He did ride the Pacific Electric cars to Avalon and 42nd Street often enough to come to like the old park. In fact, he thought it was more like a major league park than the Dodgers' first home in Los Angeles, the Memorial Coliseum. He remembers that you had to force yourself to be in a baseball mood at the Coliseum. "You were on a mound and they had a dirt infield. Otherwise it's a football stadium."

No such problem at Dodger Stadium, of course. Drysdale loved playing here and is happy to be back in the announcer's booth. He will get to the park two and a half hours before game time. During batting practice he is usually down by the cage recording an interview to be replayed during the pre-game show on the Dodgers' radio network of 36 stations. The rest of the time is spent in talking to players, checking out the media guide of the visiting team, and mentally preparing for the game. He wanted to be an announcer ever since his playing days, and working for the Dodgers again is just icing on the cake.

Don Drysdale, celebration of the 20th Anniversary of
his record 58 scoreless innings pitched, 1988

STU NAHAN

It's nearing the hour mark in Stu Nahan's KABC Talkradio pre-game show. He is sitting in the Dodger dugout. The player he just interviewed has gone back into the clubhouse as the Braves take batting practice. The engineer up in the KABC area of the press box has told him there are 30 seconds to the next commercial. It is now up to Nahan to end the segment in time for the sponsor's message to be run. He has successfully mastered an ability vital to all radio talk show hosts. He can think, plan, listen, and talk all at the same time.

The remote broadcast from the dugout is a little more complicated than speaking from his typical post in the press box. At the field level, Nahan must do without the broadcasting booth's screen that lists the name, place, and topic of the various participants on his call-in show. The headphone he must wear when away from the booth allows him to hear from his engineer through one ear while listening to what is going out over the airwaves through the other. Broadcasting from the field is worth the aggravation. For the show to succeed, Nahan must often get down to the field to interview players who cannot take the time to journey up to the press box.

Radio descriptions of baseball games has been around for half a century. Red Barber, who eventually came to the Dodgers, pioneered radio broadcasting with the Cincinnati Reds in 1935. Reluctance to give away the product made the spread of radio play-by-play for all games a slow process. By World War II, however, the practice had become more accepted. Now, all games are broadcast by radio to the home team's market. Every afternoon various broadcasters will be on the field interviewing players for their taped pre-game shows. Baseball, with its seemingly placid surface masking a dozen strategies going on at the same time, lends itself perfectly to radio, which offers more time and can appeal to the listener's imagination in a manner for which television was never intended.

Stu Nahan has worked in both mediums. He notes that television offers considerably more exposure, but very little time for creativity. He is allowed only six minutes for his nightly spot on the KTLA nighttime news. On KABC radio, he has much more time to use, and therefore a great deal more latitude in the subjects he might cover or the people he might interview.

Stu Nahan, 1988

MICKEY HATCHER – PRE-GAME

Mickey Hatcher seems like the loosest guy in uniform before a game. He is always joking with anyone available, particularly his teammates. He is one of the few players to sign autographs before a game, trading quips all the while. It's easy to forget what a talented athlete he is because he does not look the part. But this is a man who not only has spent the past nine years playing major league baseball; his senior year of high school back in Mesa, Arizona, found him on prep All-American teams in both baseball and football. At the University of Oklahoma he was second-team All-American in baseball and a starting wide receiver on the football team. His enthusiasm was evident all season long, but never more so than in the World Series. His home run and exuberant dash around the bases in Game 1 was one of the most joyous highlights of the Dodger season.

Hatcher will spend some of his pre-game time kidding the other Dodgers, pulling on Dodger video cameraman Jeff Claire's huge power cord, playing catch, and running in the outfield. That is always an amazing sight. Hatcher runs like all his body parts aren't connected quite right. If he's not starting that day, he might sign some more autographs or sit in the dugout watching whatever musicians, marching band, drill team, or acrobats are cavorting in the outfield.

But all the kidding stops when Hatcher is hitting in the cage. Then you get a good view of the engine that drives a professional athlete. He'll have it in mind if he wants to pull the ball or go to right field with it. The anger or satisfaction with the result is evident on his face and in his agonized or ecstatic comments. Not only is this his living, it is his art. Hatcher is paid to hit and he does it very well. The batting cage is serious business.

Pre-game activities done, Hatcher will once again resume his other job of keeping the team loose. Every successful team will have somebody to perform this wholly necessary function. It shouldn't be confused with not taking the game seriously. No one, not Gibson or Sax, is more intense than Mickey Hatcher. He just expresses it a little differently.

Mickey Hatcher (right) and Tim Belcher, 1988

TIM LEARY

Tim Leary was having the best season of his major league career. He had mastered the split-finger fastball and become one of the mainstays of the Dodger starting rotation. He was voted the National League Comeback Player of the Year for 1988 by the United Press International and *Sporting News*, and a poll of managers conducted by *Baseball Digest* chose him as the best-hitting pitcher in the senior circuit. In September the pitcher was even the subject of an article in his high school newspaper.

The photo well was jammed as the Dodgers fought to clinch their division. Santa Monica High School senior Luke Iwabuchi was in the well with the rest of us. His assignment from the school paper was to get some shots of Leary as he pitched. This was not the best of all possible nights for either the subject or the photographer. Leary was removed in the sixth inning. Iwabuchi had done the job he was sent to do. He sat down, pulled out his physics text book and started to read. He had his shots, he noted, and, "Hey, I've got a hell of a lot of homework."

Back in June, Leary, the hometown boy, had gone over to the box seats by the Dodger dugout because he saw an old friend. But he is now a major league star. Proximity to the stands brought over the fans. He tried to talk to his friend as he gave autographs, signing and signing in the warm afternoon sun. Most of the people who came over were boys with something for Leary to write on. Some had hats; others presented balls, gloves or programs. He good-naturedly signed whatever was put in front of him, all the time talking to an old friend.

Among the fans who came for an autograph was a pleasant-looking blond woman in a halter top and shorts. "God, he's gorgeous," she said to me. She had just faced the trauma of her thirtieth birthday and was still feeling pretty depressed about the whole thing. "He looks so young," she said. "How old do you think he is?" Leary overheard the exchange and looked up from his autographing. "I'm 29," he said, and smiled. The woman absolutely melted. She blushed as she said, "You have beautiful eyes." Leary thanked her for the compliment, signed his name on a few more pieces of paper, said good-bye to his pal, and went off to do some running in the outfield and shag fly balls while the starting lineup took batting practice. The crowd that had gathered to get an autograph dispersed. The woman went back to sit with a girlfriend, animatedly talking about what had happened.

Just another day in the life of a major league ballplayer.

Tim Leary signing autographs, 1988

"DODGER MOM"

The best time to talk to players is before the game. They are usually looser and often more approachable than after a game when they want to get home. So I always made it a point to get to the park several hours before the game. The general entrance gates are still closed, not to open until 6:00 p.m. But the first fans of the day are already lined up, waiting for the gates to go up. At the head of the parked cars, talking to everyone who stops by under her protective umbrella, is Betty Chatwood – better known as "Dodger Mom."

Betty has been a baseball fan since she was a girl. She grew up near Wrigley Field on 42nd Street. Her father often took her to Angel games, but her strongest memory of the Coast League days was when George Raft and Slapsy Maxie Rosenbloom used to park in her family's driveway because Raft hated to park his Cadillac on the gravel in the stadium parking lot. The Hollywood stars sometimes paid for the kids to go to a game. In 1937, Rosenbloom even hired a limousine to ferry Betty's whole family to San Diego for an Angel–Padres game in thanks for the parking privileges. Raising a family took up most of Betty's time by the 1950s. She became a Dodger fan when the team came west, but raising her three sons tended to keep her away from the Coliseum or Dodger Stadium and at home in Burbank. But life is an unpredictable thing, and it offered Betty Chatwood a series of heartaches. One of her sons died in childhood. A second, who worked for the Dodgers, was killed in a motorcycle accident. Several years ago, her husband also passed on. As her own family was slowly decimated, the Dodgers gradually became another family for her. She started coming to the stadium regularly in 1972, sitting in the Left Field Pavilion. She has not missed a game in the last 17 years. Her remaining son now pays for her season ticket behind home plate on the Field Level.

Betty has had lots of favorite players over the years. Near the top of the list is current Giant coach and former Dodger outfielder Dusty Baker. He was the one who started calling her "Dodger Mom." Her first post was in "Cannon Country" in the Left Field Pavilion, and she loved to watch its namesake, Jimmy Wynn, "The Toy Cannon." Ron Cey, Bill Russell, and Steve Yeager are her other favorites from the late 1970s. Now she is especially fond of Mike Scioscia and looks forward to seeing Alfredo Griffin and Willie Randolph turn double plays because it reminds her of Davey Lopes and Bill Russell. She always looks forward to games with the Astros. They knew her son and all came over to offer condolences after hearing of his death. Joe Niekro and his wife, Nancy, were especially kind.

Chances are Dodger Mom will be first at the gate in 1990, also. She is looking forward to the Dodger centennial year and all the celebration that will accompany the games. She has a hard time getting around now because of arthritis, but she still never misses a game. Betty can't wait until April, when she will get another chance to cheer on "her boys."

Betty Chatwood, "Dodger Mom," 1989

PRE-GAME SECURITY

Various branches of the constabulary are stationed throughout Dodger Stadium. The ushers will handle any sort of minor problems. They will try to quiet down a drunk, change the seat of someone causing trouble or arguing with other fans, and in general try to keep the peace. As usher Marc Proval put it, "We just try to make the place as enjoyable as possible for people."

If a paying customer is determined to make "the place" unenjoyable by his behavior, Dodger Security is called. Within the property boundaries of the stadium, Dodger Security personnel can make a citizen's arrest. The most common problem is drunkenness, and its attendant obnoxious behavior. Markedly antisocial activities will result in a trip "upstairs" to the holding cell in the upper levels of the stadium. Here, off-duty L.A.P.D. officers, who also patrol the park in plainclothes, will check the detainee for outstanding warrants. If there is one, or if the individual's behavior has earned it, he will be escorted to a city lockup by the police.

Patrick Chee is the first to point out that this rarely happens. He is stationed at the entrance to the Field Level boxes near the Left Field Pavilion. Now in his third season, Chee has learned what to look for as fans enter the park. "The main idea is to use common sense." All large bags are searched. Cans, bottles, or alcohol are not allowed into the stadium. The fan is given the option of returning it to his car or having the contraband confiscated. The point of all this is to keep lethal missiles out of the hands of potentially excitable people and thereby protect the person of players and umpires. Chee is unfailingly courteous as he checks the several thousand people who stream by him on their way into the ballpark. He is very good at defusing the potentially annoying need to search large bags.

This is the approach taken by the various security forces on hand at the stadium. The off-duty Los Angeles policemen who stand guard in the players' parking lot after the game say they love patrolling at the stadium. Officer Woody Beardsley notes, "People come out here to have fun. This isn't like working the streets at all. It's like a vacation working out here."

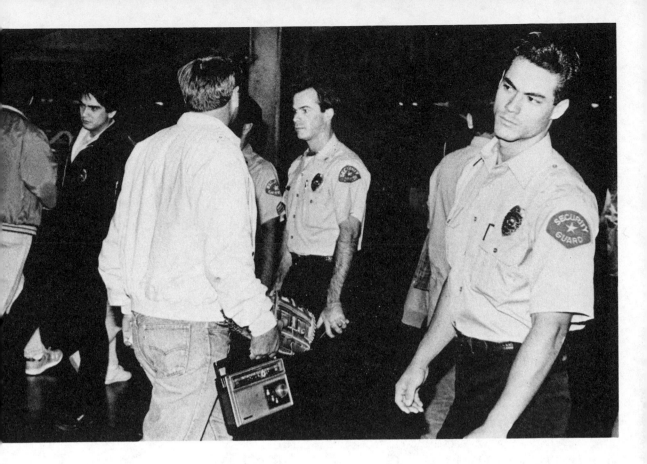

Patrick Chee (right) and other security men, 1988

THE NATIONAL ANTHEM

The pre-game repetitions are done for the day. After the visiting team finishes batting practice the cage is dismantled and stored away. The plywood planks that protect the plate area from dozens of milling pairs of spikes have all been picked up. A quick infield practice follows. Much the same as at any Little League park in America. That's part of the wonder of the game: It is so similar in everything but execution from the top of its form to the bottom.

Following batting and infield practice, the Dodgers walk back to the dressing room down a short hallway from the dugout to put on clean game uniforms. While the team is changing, Louis Basile and the grounds crew are chalking the field and raking the mound and home plate area. Several of the Dodgers are quickly back out of the dugout. Kirk Gibson and Steve Sax get in some running in the outfield. Mike Marshall warms up along the third base line with bat boy Shawn Evans. A couple of players will be signing some last-minute autographs near the Dodger dugout. Once the game starts, the autographs cease. An usher is always stationed in front of the gate that leads to the photo well and the dugout, and will chase away anyone calling to the players to sign something. In the photo well, the photographers are checking their cameras and site lines. Jeff Claire, the Diamond Vision video cameraman, has his camera on his shoulder and is walking with Jon SooHoo, the Dodger still photographer, out to center field to shoot the guest singer for the evening.

Up in the press box, Dodger public address announcer Nick Nickson asks the fans to stand for the National Anthem. All around him, members of the working press are getting to their feet. Two rows behind him, Nancy Hefley is seated at her organ and ready to play. The singer has entered the center-field gate and is standing next to a microphone. Both team's players are lined up next to the dugout or in the outfield, caps off, and held over their hearts. Throughout the always crowded stadium, fans are rising. The Anthem will be sung, and another game will begin.

Tim Leary singing the National Anthem, 1988

PART TWO: THE GAME

The National Anthem has ended. The Dodgers take the field to the cheers of their fans. The game is starting.

Like all baseball games, it will run on its own schedule. The clock is unimportant, only the coming and going of innings matter. If at the end of the regulation nine innings the game is tied, the teams will go on playing until someone wins.

At the least, baseball can be appreciated for the poetry of movement of the men playing: the fluidity of Orel Hershiser's delivery or the graceful strides of John Shelby as he chases down a flyball. Even the casual fan will get excited by a close play at the plate or a home run. The dedicated fan sees much more. How is the outfield shading the hitter? The batter is a contact hitter and the man on first base is fairly slow afoot. Is this a good time for a hit-and-run play? Has the pitcher recovered from the sore arm he had earlier in the season? How is he setting up the hitter? Baseball is so deceptive. Half the time it seems to consist of nothing more than the pitcher and catcher tossing the ball back and forth. But no matter how innocuous the action seems, it only masks the innumerable strategies involved with each man at bat.

Baseball is the national pastime because of the insight it offers into American traditions. There is constant individual activity within a group context. Individuals constantly are challenged and have to prove themselves. It might be an at bat, a groundball and the subsequent throw to first, or a pitch. Whatever the case, it is one man on the spot. It is the reaffirmation of the most sacred of our national beliefs – the democratic emphasis on the individual.

There is much more going on in the ballpark than the game on the field. Lots of people are supplementing their income by selling peanuts, beer, or souvenirs. The press box is full, as are the photographer's wells. Ushers are giving directions, janitors are sweeping up trash on the concourses. Tens of thousands of fans are watching the game. This is one of 81 games that will be played at Dodger Stadium this season. It might be important in the standings, it might not. It may be a cliffhanger, it may be a blowout. But whatever the outcome, it will contain moments of beauty.

Mike Marshall, 1989

THE MOST VALUABLE PLAYER

Kirk Gibson had an outstanding offensive year. His .290 batting average was 11th in the National League, while he was 9th in home runs and 16th in R.B.I.s. Good numbers. But not what you would normally expect of a someone voted the League's Most Valuable Player. This year's award seemed to be given as much for leadership and perceived player impact as for raw data.

The pre-season sun-black-in-the-hat practical joke has become as much a part of Dodger lore as Mickey Owen's missed third strike in the 1941 World Series. Gibson's angrily stalking off the field is generally credited with setting an aggressive, serious tone for the 1988 season. He was generally presented in the press as someone who preferred his meat raw. As the story went, his fierce dedication to winning and intense style of play lifted a team full of quiche-eating beach boys to the championship level.

This is an insult to the dedication and professionalism of the rest of the Dodgers. Gibson is the first one to deride such talk. "That's just something you people [sportswriters] made up. People here always wanted to win. This year they put together a team that could win." Tommy Lasorda agrees. "We won this year because we've got a new cast of characters. Our bullpen is better, our offense is better, our defense is better." Steve Sax commented that this year's team "has a depth we just lacked last year."

Lasorda notes all the other factors that led to his team's winning the world championship in 1988. But it is clear that Kirk Gibson occupies a special place in his heart. It was late in the season and the Dodgers had just beat the Braves on a ninth-inning Mike Marshall single that drove home a running Gibson. Journalists crowded around Marshall after the game, only to hear him say he knew he needed a hit since "Gibby" got such a good jump and could score from first with the way he was running. A few minutes later, Lasorda was just wrapping up an anti-drug speech for a televised post-game interview. Gibson walked into the manager's office looking as intense as usual. Happy, but still intense. Lasorda asked the interviewer to turn the tape back on. The TV crew complied, and Lasorda gave another impassioned address on how grateful he was to Detroit for sending him Gibson. All this on a night when Marshall got the game-winning hit in the bottom of the ninth inning.

Kirk Gibson did not win the pennant for the Dodgers by force of personality. But he was the catalyst around which the 1988 team was formed.

Kirk Gibson hitting a single up the middle, 1988

KIRK GIBSON IN LOS ANGELES

Kirk Gibson was having a poor night. He struck out with a man on base, and now he had misplayed a ball in the outfield. As he walked back to the dugout after the inning, a fan yelled out, "Ya blew it, Gibson." The outfielder stared at him, looking back over his shoulder as he walked. The fan elbowed his companion, said, "Hey, I got to him, huh?" After the Dodger half inning, Gibson returned to left field. He slowly walked past the heckler, still staring. No more comments from the stands.

Gibson is an intense guy. Whether he is glaring at boorish young men, stretching behind the cage prior to batting practice, walking to the plate to hit, instructing fans in the rules for getting an autograph, or bringing his small son into Tommy Lasorda's office after a game, the mood seems to only change by small degree. Whatever he is doing is being done with serious intent.

The fans in Los Angeles eat this up. Most East Coast critics look at Los Angeles, note the lack of winter snow, debilitating summer humidity, and people maniacally saying "getoutaheh," and assume the whole city does nothing but spend its time soaking up sun rays and sipping mineral water. What is inevitably missed in all this is how radically the city has grown and changed in the past 20 years. Palm trees are still here and snow isn't, but the general pace of the city has escalated drastically.

The easiest way for the native Angeleno to come face to face with his aggressive nature is to drive a car in another city and watch the blood drain from the faces of the non-Californians sitting next to him. What passes for normal driving procedure in Los Angeles is seen as pathological aggression any other place except New York or San Francisco. It should also be kept in mind that the city is the home of the entertainment industry, the single most competitive business in the country.

The knit-browed intensity that Kirk Gibson brings to everything he does may have seemed hopelessly out of place in Los Angeles to those living east of San Bernardino. In the Los Angeles of myth, it would be. But that place is gone, if it ever existed at all. Gibson fits the L.A. that has emerged in the late 20th century perfectly. It is no surprise that he was so immediately adopted by Dodger fans as the ideal symbol of what they wanted their team to be.

Kirk Gibson, striking out, 1988

OREL HERSHISER

Orel Hershiser stands next to his locker answering questions from a crowd of reporters. He has won again. Another shutout. This time against the hapless Atlanta Braves. He is closing in on Don Drysdale's 20-year-old record of 58 scoreless innings in a row as the Dodgers come closer to clinching the championship of the National League West. Hershiser is in his uniform pants and gray undershirt. He looks so thin. Just a tall, skinny guy with a very serious demeanor. No challenging of the reporters as is typical of Kirk Gibson. Not the reserve of John Shelby, either. Simply a pleasant young man talking about his day at work.

But how he can throw a baseball. As with all successful pitchers, it is not so much the speed of his ball but its movement that makes him dominating. The choirboy exterior is a perfect mask for the desire that is within. Tommy Lasorda nicknamed Hershiser "Bulldog." It may have been one of the manager's many attempts at motivating his players. But it is an accurate description of the single-minded approach the pitcher has when he takes the mound. The two shutout leaders make such a perfect contrast, Hershiser with the calm exterior and seething interior, Drysdale 6 feet 6 inches of pure, obvious aggression. The side-arm whipping motion. The menacing look from the mound. Seeming to want to rip the throat out of anyone who got a hit off him. But both of them Dodgers. Hershiser is a player with a sense of the history of the game. He knew exactly whose record he was challenging and that the man was in the broadcasting booth. For his part, Drysdale is firmly ensconced in the Hall of Fame. He is secure in his talent and his contribution to baseball. He appreciates his record, but knows it does not define either him or his career. He means it when he says he's glad the record has stayed in the Dodger family.

Orel Hershiser broke the record in the tenth inning of his last start of the 1988 season. But Hershiser did not stop with setting a new scoreless-inning record. He went on to be named Most Valuable Player in both the National League Championship Series and the World Series. He also was awarded the National League Cy Young Award and got the chance to sing on *The Tonight Show* with Johnny Carson. Some year. Proof positive that aggression and desire can sometimes wear a gentle mask.

Orel Hershiser pitching against the Astros, 1988

AFTER THE AWARDS

Orel and Jamie Hershiser were finally able to take a small vacation. The early off-season following the 1988 World Series triumph had been an endlessly involving round of dinners, awards, and speaking engagements. When they were finally able to create some time for themselves, like so many other Southern California couples, they headed north up the coast toward the Big Sur and Monterey. On the first night of the trip, the Hershisers decided to see a movie. Small town on the Monterey Peninsula. Late movie. In 1987 this may have called for an autograph to an observant fan. But this was the winter of 1988. Orel Hershiser was the biggest thing in baseball. When the couple left the theater, the local television station's truck was outside. A reporter approached the pitcher with his cameraman and asked for an interview. Hershiser noted the lateness of the hour and arranged to speak with the fellow the next morning – on the second day of his vacation.

It is no easy task to be a celebrity in America. When fame descends on someone, it is overwhelming. Suddenly everyone seems to recognize you. Local and national news organizations want to speak to you. Charities want your help. Seminars full of salesmen or business leaders want you to come and motivate them. On and on. The hero of the moment must pay with his private life. There are newspapers and air time to be sold as a man rises or as he falls. It seems to matter so little to the media as they swarm about, desperate for an angle on this latest story.

But Orel Hershiser weathered the storm, marriage and sanity intact. He did several commercials, lots of interviews, and even wrote a book before the 1989 season began. His new contract may have made him a multi-millionaire, but that didn't help his win-loss record. As the Dodgers sank slowly in the west, his winning percentage went along with them. Pitching is often said to be 90 percent of the game. An overstatement, as the Dodgers proved this year. Hershiser's record may have fallen to 14–14, but his 2.31 E.R.A. was almost equal to 1988's 2.26. Tommy Lasorda argued that the pitcher's stuff was still of Cy Young Award caliber. His record looked bad because the team couldn't score him any runs.

Frustration all around in 1989. At least the book did well. It is due out in paperback in time for the 1990 season.

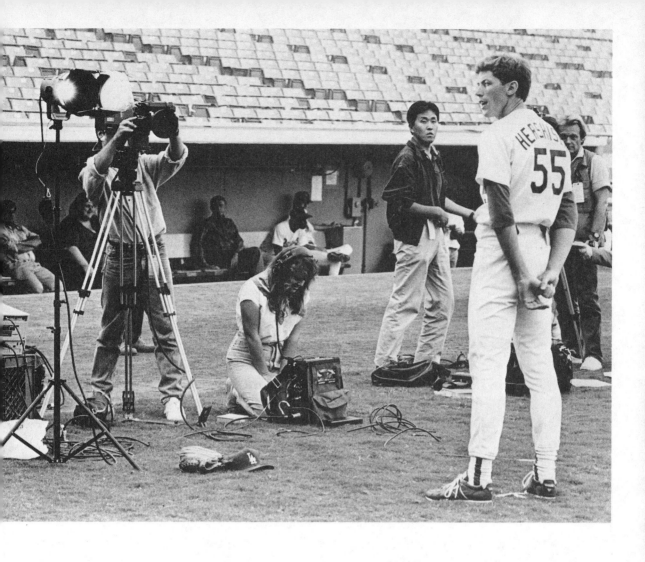

Orel Hershiser, 1988

THE ENTHUSIASM OF STEVE SAX

Steve Sax plays major league baseball like everyone on your Pony League All Star team was convinced they would play if they someday made the grade. He seems to relish every moment of the experience. Sax is perpetually in motion, manic with enthusiasm. He paces excitedly in the dugout waiting for the game to start. When it is finally time, he bursts out onto the field. John Shelby glides smoothly as he runs to center field. Mickey Hatcher churns determinedly over to first. But Sax darts out to second base.

Sax is the same eager, effervescent presence whether he's signing autographs or around the batting cage. He runs in and out of the cage. He dashes around the bases after taking his cuts. Sax is very straightforward when answering a reporter's questions as he waits for his next turn at bat. But he is never still. He flicks the bat around, stretches, watches the pitcher. The man practically vibrates with energy. The previous day had featured a pre-game ceremony featuring 35 junior high school bands and drill teams. After performing, they took their seats in the Right Field Pavilion. The stadium reverberated with their screams the whole game, but the volume rose to rock concert decibels whenever Steve Sax came to bat. When asked about the way girls often scream when he's at the plate, Sax smiled. "Oh, yeah," he laughed. "Well, that's nice. It's great to hear that." He has the same attitude toward signing autographs. It's all a part of the game, and so long as he doesn't feel exploited, he enjoys it.

The kind of enthusiasm Mickey Hatcher and Steve Sax have been blessed with is usually referred to as "boyish" – as if it were undignified for a grown man to take so much enjoyment in what he is doing. Sax certainly does not back down from questions about his remarkable energy level. In fact, he considers them foolish. "I'm playing a game that I love, get to compete in the major leagues, and have a wonderful family. All I have to do to get enthused is wake up in the morning."

Steve Sax warming up, 1988

MIKE MARSHALL

It is 6:00. Mark Cresse is collecting the balls around home plate with the help of the next group of batting-practice hitters. He will soon be pitching to Mike Scioscia, Kirk Gibson, John Shelby, and Mike Marshall. Down in the Left Field Pavilion and Field Level boxes, the just arriving fans are on their feet, gloves on. If any balls are going to make it to the stands, it should be from this group. Sure enough, Mike Marshall parks one. A man in the pavilion catches the home run. He yells across to the fans in the more expensive box seats that he will sell the ball for $3.00. There's a taker.

The guy who caught the ball runs down the pavilion steps to the corridor leading to the base of the field boxes. A fan in the stands tosses down a five-dollar bill. "Keep the change," he calls as the ball is tossed up to him. Sitting down, souvenir in hand, he says to his wife, "Maybe I can get Mike to sign it for me."

The flow of information from all varieties of media have broken the wall of mystery that traditionally separated celebrities from their fans. Ballplayers, movie stars, rock singers, or famous murderers are inevitably called by their first names. There is a supposed familiarity implied by this informality.

The fan with the ball might be one of the people along the fence of the player's parking lot calling, "Mike, Mike, just one. Hey Mike!" Or he could have been one of the fans loudly requesting that the outfielder take off his cap and display his new buzz cut. Anytime Marshall made the last out in an inning and waited, hatless, for his cap and glove to arrive from the dugout, the fans cheered.

Mike Marshall never did anything to encourage these responses. He didn't have to. He is a first-string, major league ballplayer. A celebrity. In the late 20th century, fans have come to feel a proprietary interest in their idols. The supposed familiarity and demands for attention come with the territory. They are as much a part of the game as the uniforms and gloves.

Mike Marshall waiting for his hat and glove, 1988

MIKE SCIOSCIA

It is a night in mid-September. Mike Scioscia has just hit a home run off the Braves' John Smoltz to win the game for the Dodgers, 2–0. "Iron Mike" has made his reputation for his contact hitting and defensive work. No one in the National League is any better at blocking a runner off the plate. Steve Yeager, his predecessor, also made his reputation for his defense. But he was forever chafing at being seen as one-dimensional. Yeager wanted to be compared to Johnny Bench. Mike Scioscia is not self-promotional. He is one of those athletes easy to overlook because he just does his job. He isn't colorful or loud. Just talented and steady.

A close look at the photograph will show something else about Scioscia. He is wearing a high-top baseball shoe on his left foot to relieve the pressure on the calcium deposits in his heel. In the best tradition of catchers everywhere, the most stoic position on a baseball field, he is going about his work in spite of the pain.

After circling the bases, Scioscia was met at home plate by his teammates. The catcher had hit a game-winning home run. Guys were excited. Had this been a game 20 years ago this would have been an occasion celebrated by hand-clasps, pats on the back, and happy expressions. But this is the late 1980s. The Dodgers, led by the always exuberant Tommy Lasorda, pummel Scioscia, hug him, high-five him, yell, and in general whip themselves into a public frenzy. This is completely new behavior for American men.

One of the biggest problems Sergio Leone had with the Italian actors he was using in his "spaghetti Westerns," like *Hang 'Em High* and *High Plains Drifter*, was getting them to not wave their hands around when they talked. Americans, especially cowboys, just did not talk like that. They were quiet, laconic, withdrawn. Our most celebrated male personalities have fit this same mold, Joe DiMaggio being the perfect example from the baseball world. Something is happening to change the equation. American men are being freed from the straitjacket of unemotionality. It might be the result of changes in modern women, the loosening of dress and behavioral codes that is a heritage of the 1960s, or the technological nature of modern life. Whatever the cause, by the late 1980s American men who are engaged in demonstrably masculine pastimes are allowed to display public emotion without fans' eyebrows being raised.

Mike Scioscia hitting a home run, 1988

MICKEY HATCHER – GAME

Orel Hershiser felt that the main difference between the Dodger teams that had failed in 1986 and '87 and the champions of 1988 was that major leaguers were filling in whenever one of the starters was hurt rather than minor leaguers. Dave Anderson played brilliantly when Alfredo Griffin had his hand fractured by a Dwight Gooden pitch on May 21st. Rick Dempsey, who sat in Vice-President Fred Claire's office for two hours to ask for a tryout after being released by the Indians, filled in admirably as catcher and pinch-hitter. Mickey Hatcher, a castoff from the Twins, played first, third, and the outfield. He also did a lot of pinch-hitting.

This is certainly one of the toughest assignments in the big leagues. To sit on the bench all night long, only to be called on to produce late in the game, with victory or defeat often the outcome. Naturally Hatcher would rather play every day. The decision, however, is not his to make. After arriving at the ballpark at 3:00 or so, Hatcher will check the starting lineup. Regardless of what it says, he will do some work in the weight room. If he is not starting, he assumes his role will be to pinch-hit. After pre-game hitting, running, and shagging, he will spend the first five innings on the bench. About the sixth inning Hatcher will take a few cuts against the mechanical pitcher in the batting cage under the stands down the hall from the Dodger clubhouse. The idea here is to keep your timing. Obviously the machine is no match for game conditions.

After taking his cuts, Hatcher returns to the bench. On most nights he will keep up a steady line of chatter. Like Jay Johnstone and Fernando Valenzuela, he plays the vital role of helping to keep teammates loose. Certainly no one outside vaudeville has a more mobile face than Mickey Hatcher. But if it seems likely he might pinch-hit, the joviality is down, the concentration up. Most of the time he will be carrying his bat in the dugout in the late innings. "It helps me keep my mind on hitting," Hatcher explains.

It certainly worked well. In 1988 Mickey Hatcher was the leading Dodger pinch-hitter, and sixth most effective in the National League, with a .316 average in 38 attempts.

Mickey Hatcher waiting to pinch-hit, 1988

RICK DEMPSEY

Extra innings against the Braves. Bottom of the eleventh inning. Rick Dempsey, who played his first major league game for the Minnesota Twins 20 years ago, is at bat. He has been forty years old for four days. In 1988 he came to the Dodgers to ask for a tryout after being unconditionally released by the Indians. He won the job and wants to keep it. Tonight helped the campaign. He hit a home run to win it for the Dodgers.

After the game, Dempsey was standing in front of his locker, surrounded by reporters. After the standard questions about what type of pitch it was, how it felt, etc., talk turned to his future. Dempsey noted that he was playing behind one of the best catchers in the National League in Mike Scioscia. He is a member in good standing of the Stuntmen, and even if he is not starting, feels he has to be ready when called upon. Tonight he was. He also tagged two runners out in ferocious collisions at the plate. "I feel like I'm on a roll. The hits are coming and I've been calling the games well. I feel I can still play and know I have to convince the Dodgers that I'm right."

When asked about some of the differences in baseball since the days he broke in, Dempsey noted that for the first time in big league history, there were three active catchers over the age of forty. He is in the company of Bob Boone of the Royals and Carlton Fisk of the White Sox. He argued that all three of them benefited from their years of experience. Catchers are never hired for speed; their key contribution is in running the game. Dempsey believes this improves over time.

A further lure for staying with the team is playing with the Dodgers. Dempsey notes that major league baseball itself "is an exciting life style." Playing for his hometown team just makes it even better. Regardless of where he was playing, Dempsey kept his home in Los Angeles. His friends and family are here, and returning to play at Dodger Stadium "is a dream come true. It may have come late, but it's better late than never."

When playing Little League and Pony League baseball in the San Fernando Valley, Rick Dempsey often imagined himself batting with the game on the line at Dodger Stadium. On September 17, 1989, he did just that and won it with a home run. Dreams can come true. One other dream Dempsey has is to play major league ball in four decades. He played as hard as he could in 1989. It is now up to the Dodger hierarchy to decide.

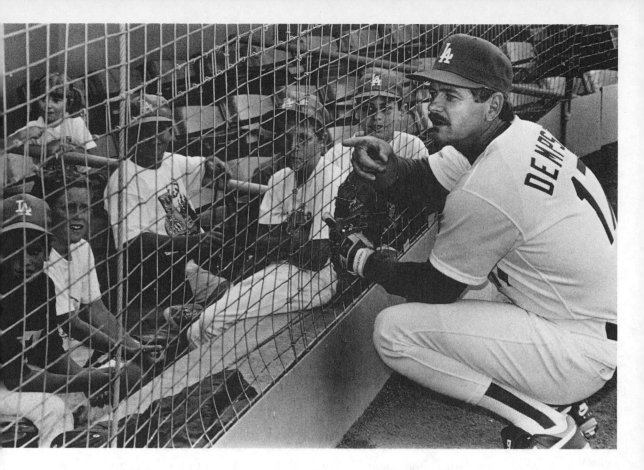

Rick Dempsey, talking to his cousin's Little League team, 1989

FERNANDO'S ORDEAL

He had not missed a start in seven seasons. Year after year he was good for well over 200 innings pitched. From 1981 to 1986, he pitched $7\frac{2}{3}$ scoreless innings in six All Star games. His initial seasons brought Latino fans to Dodger Stadium like never before. But in 1987, the train went off the track for Fernando Valenzuela.

He broke even that year, going 14 and 14. He tied for the National League lead in complete games, third in innings pitched, and tied for fourth in strikeouts. But he had his highest total of walks, wild pitches, hits and home runs allowed, and E.R.A. An odd year for one of the strongest competitors in the league.

1988 was much worse. The team was doing well, but Fernando was obviously in trouble. Tests eventually disclosed a stretched anterior capsule in his pitching shoulder. Valenzuela was placed on the 21-day disabled list on July 31. This turned out to be a little optimistic. He did not pitch again until September 26, making two appearances late in the season. Fernando was not on the Dodgers' post-season roster. His place on the pitching staff was taken by Ramon Martinez.

1989 started slowly for the pitcher. He did not win a game until June, almost exactly one year after his last victory. But Fernando got stronger as the season wore on. In an off year for the team, he finally wound up with a 10–13 record. Not a career best of any sort, but certainly back on the right track.

Valenzuela came back through sheer determination. All the while he was on the D.L., he regularly performed all the strengthening exercises recommended by Dodger physical therapist Pat Screnar. Meanwhile, he still worked out with the team. No pitching, obviously, but he was out there everyday shagging balls, fielding grounders, and catching balls for fungo hitters. He cheered the team on from the bench, and in general remained an integral part of the Dodgers even if he could not play. Fernando also continued to play a role in the community. He gives a lot of his free time to the "Be Smart, Stay in School" program that rewards kids who have perfect attendance, and urges those thinking of dropping out to reconsider.

It is this determination to succeed, team spirit, and community spirit that made Fernando Valenzuela one of the most popular players ever to wear a Dodger uniform. The days of "Fernando Mania" may be past, but the mention of his name still never fails to draw a cheer at Dodger Stadium.

Fernando Valenzuela, 1989

DIFFERENT AGENDAS

One of the ways baseball writers are luckier than other sportswriters is the century-old backlog of stories they have to draw on when it's an off day. One of the Dodgers' most honored legends is their longstanding rivalry with the Giants. It started during the time when the two National League teams represented the same city. No matter how lousy the Brooklyn teams of the 1920s and '30s may have been, their fans could always find pleasure in booing the Giants.

To some extent, the rivalry followed the two teams across the country in 1958. But the reason for it shifted. It is impossible to recreate what started as a subway rivalry when the two teams are connected by 400 miles of interstate highways. What kept it going in the early 1960s was the competitive nature of the two teams. The Giants and the Dodgers were constantly neck and neck in the National League pennant races.

But this certainly does not stop reporters from asking even new additions to the Dodgers about the rivalry. Eddie Murray is a native of Los Angeles, and is familiar with the history of the conflict between the Dodgers and the Giants. But he is a professional baseball player, not a fan or a writer, and his perspective is different. He notes that all the ink spilled over the rivalry and the past is a reporter's question, not a ballplayer's concern. His pride as an athlete spurs him to concentrate on every game and "do the best I can." The opponent makes a difference in terms of how they play and if there is a pennant race at stake, but what happened 50 years ago across a continent does not. "I come here to play. It's my job." He is concerned with who is pitching today, not play-off games in 1951 or 1962.

The same concentration on the job at hand enters into Mike Scioscia's attitude toward his job behind the plate. The Dodgers have had excellent catchers going back four decades. Roy Campanella, John Roseboro, and Steve Yeager were all leading practitioners of the catcher's art. Scioscia is aware of this past, of course. He followed baseball as a boy. But it is not something that is talked about among the players themselves all that much. "It's great to be a part of that kind of tradition, but the past doesn't put pressure on me."

Like Eddie Murray, his concentration is on the present and helping the team to win today's game. They both understand fans' interest in the past and the desire of writers to ask them their feelings about something they had no part in winning or losing. But it is not part of their game plan. Their time is now.

Mike Scioscia meets the press, 1989

JOE AMALFITANO

Joe Amalfitano, the Dodgers' third base coach, has been involved with major league baseball since 1954. He, like Sandy Koufax, was one of those unfortunate bonus babies in the 1950s who received over $6,000 to sign and were forced to occupy space on major league benches for two years before they could they be sent to the minors. He had a ten-year career with three teams. After retiring in 1967, he coached for several national league teams and managed the Cubs in 1980 and 1981. He signed on with the Dodgers in 1983. Pre-game finds Amalfitano hitting endless groundballs to the infielders. But he doesn't join the team once it leaves the field following batting practice. He can usually be found in the Dodger dugout, watching the visiting team take fielding practice. As third base coach, he will pay particular attention to how the outfielders are throwing. If one of the fielders seems to be favoring his arm, or unusually erratic, "we may decide to test that man," he says.

Amalfitano believes in "knowledge, preparation, and execution" as the reasons for winning ballgames. The execution is up to the players, but the knowledge of how aggressive to be on the basepaths comes from scout's reports, watching the player in the past, and watching some more before the game. The knowledge will be passed on to the players in the pre-game clubhouse meeting.

One of the primary considerations of a third base coach is how aggressive to be with a runner. Part of this will have to do with the speed of the individual headed toward third, of course. Other factors include the strength and accuracy of the outfielder's arm, how quickly he can field and release the ball, and how he charges a base hit. While all this is running through his mind, Amalfitano also has to remember who is pitching. How is his control? What sort of E.R.A. does he have? Also, what inning is it? Have the Dodgers been winning lately, or scored many runs? Does the team need a good shaking up?

The third base coach has been studying outfielders for 35 years. During his playing career, Amalfitano was particularly impressed by the outfielding of his teammate Willie Mays and by Dodger right fielder Carl Furillo, the "Reading Rifle." Today, the outfielders whom he most admires are the Mets' Kevin McReynolds and the Pirates' Andy Van Slyke. All of these players had the aggressive charge, quick release, and accuracy of throw the marks the best defensive outfielders.

Joe Amalfitano, late afternoon, 1989

MIKE BRITO

Every game televised from Dodger Stadium features Mike Brito in a supporting role. He is the fellow with the Jugs speed gun and large cigar standing in the dugout seats to the right of the catcher. He will chart every pitch thrown during the game, noting its type, speed, and location. Once the game is over, he can be found in the Dodgers' offices completing his detailed report on the kind of game the pitchers threw. It is as important to note the way Dodger hurlers performed as it is to detail how the visitors tried to get the home team out.

Brito is a special assignments scout. When the team is at home, he will be at his post behind the plate. When the Dodgers go on the road, he will sometimes accompany them, but generally he will be sent to another major league city to report on a future opponent or to a minor league town to chart the progress of players in the system.

Scouting is his job now, but Mike Brito has done most everything in baseball. He learned to play the game in Havana, Cuba, his hometown. He played twelve years of minor league ball, reaching the Triple-A level. During the Dodgers' off season he is a manager for Guaymas in the Mexican winter leagues. Brito notes that managing is the "most difficult" job he has had yet in baseball, but it is also his favorite. He disputes the notion that the Mexican leagues are inferior to the Caribbean leagues. Teams from his league have represented Mexico well at the winter-league world series – called the Caribbean Series – held in February. Among the many teams he has seen in his travels in Latin America is the Cuban National Team. He looks forward to the day when Cubans will again be allowed to play in the United States. He is convinced that at least six members of that team have the talent to play in the majors.

He would love to scout Cuban prospects someday, but so far "the best discovery I ever had," he says, was found playing for the Silao team of the Central League of Mexico. Brito had gone to scout a shortstop on the opposing team, but his eye was caught by the rookie pitcher for Silao, Fernando Valenzuela. After a season at Yucatán, Fernando came to the Dodgers and rapidly became one of their most popular players. In his first year, he became the first player in major league history to win both the Rookie of the Year and Cy Young Awards. Nine years later, he has won a total of 130 games for the team. Brito became more closely linked with his discovery than is common with most scouts. In Fernando's first couple of years, the bilingual Brito helped translate for him on interviews while the pitcher learned English.

Mike Brito, with a speed gun, 1989

THE VIDEO CAMERAMEN

Frank Coll has a problem. He is chief engineer for Video Tape Enterprises and one of his camera lenses is acting up. He is sitting on the concrete outside the V.T.E. trailer in the Dodger parking lot. It is obvious a quick fix is not in the cards for the recalcitrant lens. This is a $40,000 piece of equipment, so he is loathe to try to repair it outside the shop. Another lens will have to be sent over to use for today's game with the Astros.

V.T.E. uses seven cameras for an average game. Most of their tape is used for local feeds. Tonight's game will be relayed back to Houston and shown live locally on the Z Channel cable network. Highlights will also be used on many of the local news programs. When one of the games they are covering is to be shown on national television, the network will usually rent V.T.E.'s equipment but use their own cameramen.

Jeff Claire works independently of V.T.E.'s men. He is one of the video cameramen who work directly for the Dodgers. Their images will appear on the Diamond Vision screen in left field. He is in his fourth season at the stadium and has grown adept at picking out likely fans to show on the screen during the singing of "Take Me Out to the Ballgame" during the seventh-inning stretch.

Experience has helped Claire develop a much keener sense of where the ball is at any given time. This is an absolute prerequisite for anyone on the field without a glove. Claire found this out the hard way. It was his fifth day on the job and the cameraman was panning the stands as he had been instructed. The next thing he knew he was on the bottom of the photo well with the camera on top of him and a souvenir baseball lying next to him. The line drive left an imprint of its threads on his thigh for the next three months. More soberingly, it came within inches of leaving him a soprano for life. Certainly enough to enliven any man's senses.

Stephen Chacon is next to Jeff Claire in the photo well. He has been sent to Dodger Stadium to collect individual video clips on several players for use on ABC's coverage of the National League Championship series. He has covered the Dodgers all season, but was caught by surprise today. This morning he was taping vice-presidential candidate Dan Quayle when word came through that he had to get over to the stadium. There was no time to change the Boston Red Sox uniform shirt he was wearing. This, of course, brought a good deal of derision his way from the Dodgers, and also served to embarrass Chacon. "Hey, I bleed Dodger blue," he protested. "My grandfather was buried with his Dodger hat. I never would have worn this if I knew I was coming to the stadium."

Jeff Claire, video cameraman, 1988

TIM RUE, JOHN SOOHOO, AND THE LAKERS

Photographers have little to do between innings. Confined to the photo wells near the dugouts, they will exchange gossip about shooting, check out the fans, and worry about deadlines. Tim Rue shoots for the Associated Press. He has to have his film up in the A.P. darkroom near the press box by 9:30 so he can make a decision about which shot to use to represent the game. Some nights can be tough. Baseball is a hard game to cover with a camera. Even the game's winning moments are not always photogenic. Tonight has been one of those nights. It's 9:15 and Tim is hoping for something, anything, to take a picture of. "Jeez," he laments to the other photographers, also waiting for something gripping to shoot, "all I've got is a guy sliding into second, and it wasn't even a close play."

Jon SooHoo works for both the Dodgers and as a stringer for U.P.I. He takes most of the pictures you see in *Dodger Scorecard Magazine* and *Dodger Yearbook*. These pictures for the team are always in color, usually taken during the day, and featuring a single player. U.P.I., on the other hand, is aimed at a national audience, and wants "a hard core action shot." This means Jon will do a lot of shooting as the game progresses. SooHoo likes his work with the Dodgers, but through his association with Andy Bernstein's sports photography studio he shoots all the various local sports. His favorite is football, because "there's constant action. Much easier to photograph."

Tonight's game against the Astros was not only going slowly, it was also in direct competition with the Lakers–Pistons basketball championship game. The crowd was smaller than usual, and the two photographers, sports fans to the core, spent their time between innings watching the Laker game on their pocket Watchman televisions. When they noticed me taking their picture, Tim said, "For God's sake, don't forget to mention in the caption that this is between innings. We're at work, you know."

Tim Rue and Jon SooHoo in the photo well, between innings, 1988

VIN SCULLY

Like many of my grammar school contemporaries in the time of all-daylight World Series games, I often found myself with some nagging sickness in early October. At home, I was always disappointed when Vin Scully was not at the microphone for the Fall Classic. As a kid, I listened to him nightly as he and Jerry Doggett announced the games from the Coliseum press box. Listening to the World Series, I always wondered if it was simple familiarity that made Scully sound so much better than whoever else was at the mike. Apparently it wasn't. In 1982 he began announcing sports on the network level. The same year, he was inducted into the announcer's section of the Baseball Hall of Fame in Cooperstown, New York. He is among only thirteen men so honored in the 60-plus-year history of baseball broadcasting.

Scully grew up in the Bronx, within easy walking distance of the Polo Grounds. The future broadcaster saw lots of games through the Knot Hole Gangs established for kids by the Police Athletic League and the Catholic Youth Organization. His first big league broadcasting job came with the cross-borough rivals over in Brooklyn in 1950. He remembers Ebbets Field for its intimacy. "Even if the crowd was small, you were always aware of it." Eddie Battin and the "Dodger Sym-phony" were audible all over the park. So was the Cookie Lavageto fan who used to let air shriek out of a balloon and yell, "Cookie!" when his hero came to bat. Hilda Chester and her cow bell are famous in Dodger lore. But Vin doesn't so much remember the clanging as he does her grating voice. One afternoon, while 8,000 fans were watching a ballgame and Scully was trying to describe it over the radio, he heard that familiar voice rise up over the general hubbub of the ballpark and grate out, "Vin Scully, I love you!" The embarrassed young man at the microphone tried to go on with his work. All that got him was the bellowed command to, "Look at me when I'm talking to you!"

The Coliseum had none of Ebbets Field's communal spirit. Joe Amalfitano remembers that when a visiting team first got a look at the make-do park, "The hitters were all excited and the pitchers were all squawkin'." Scully remembers the fans as being very responsive to having a team of their own, but just seemed to be lost in the acreage of the huge football stadium. The one enduring baseball legacy of that stadium is the cavalry charge played by Corny Johnson at the games. The sound and the resulting "Charge!" yell of the crowd went out over the radio, and is now heard all over the country.

Dodger Stadium is too big to allow much of an individual notice of any one fan, but Scully notes it is one of the best parks in the majors from the standpoint of sight lines. Unlike Wrigley Field in Chicago, or Jack Murphy Stadium in San Diego, you never lose sight of the ball from the announcer's booth. Plus, it is so immaculate all the time. Scully points out that the stadium is owned by the team, and this spurs on an effort to keep it in pristine shape: "This is someone's home. The Dodgers live here."

Vin Scully, preparing the post-game wrap-up, 1989

SEASON AND OTHER TICKET HOLDERS

A common criticism of Los Angeles sports fans is that they will only support their teams when they are winning. This may be true of the professional football, basketball, and hockey teams, but it does not apply to its baseball team. Los Angeles loves the Dodgers, and has ever since they came west in 1958. The team has eight of the top ten attendance marks. The Dodgers may have finished second to last in their division two years running, but they attracted 3,023,208 fans in 1986 and 2,797,409 in 1987. For 1988 the figure was 2,980,262, just shy of their eighth three million attendance season. The 1987 Mets and Cardinals are the only other teams in baseball history to have reached that plateau. The Dodgers limit the number of season ticket holders to 27,000. Even at that, there is a waiting list. The Harter family got its season tickets early in the game. Glen Harter loved baseball, and was just as anxious as the ballplayers to get the team out of the Coliseum. In 1961 he came to the still uncompleted Chavez Ravine park, was shown around, and chose two seats in the first row, just to the left of the Dodger dugout. Twenty-six years later those same two seats are still in the family.

Gary Harter has gone to thousands of games over the years. Two of his favorite memories are the 1977 Dodgers with Steve Garvey, Dusty Baker, Ron Cey, and Reggie Smith all hitting over 30 home runs, and Sandy Koufax signing the cast on his broken arm when Gary was eight. His wife, Kendis, is also a longtime Dodger fan. She had to come up with a new favorite player when Bob Welch was traded to Oakland. Steve Sax took his place in her cheering. Gary has always favored outfielders. Dusty Baker was number one to him in the past. Now he follows Kirk Gibson.

Meanwhile, up in the Reserved Level, well down the first base line, 36 people from Marymount High School near Westwood are cheering on the home team. This is the third year in a row a group of faculty and staff from the school has attended a game. One of the organizers of the event is math teacher Marilyn Bennett. Baseball was a new game to her when she arrived in the States from England thirteen years ago. She vaguely understood the rules from having played rounders (the English parent of baseball) in school, but it took the patient counseling of her friend, Stan Saunders, to make the strategy of the game intelligible. Marilyn is now a dedicated fan, following the daily fortunes of the Dodgers through the summer, and waiting impatiently for the long baseball-less winter to finally end.

Kendis and Gary Harter, 1988

STADIUM NIGHTS

Lisa del Duca and Dolly Kejmar came over to ask why I was taking pictures. I told them I was looking for some Dodger fans. They said I had found two. They don't come to the game quite as often as the Harters and the view is not as good up on the General Admission level, but they are rabid fans. "Oh, we just love the Dodgers," Dolly assured me. "Especially Steve Sax," Lisa pointed out.

Top Deck, General Admission. Up in the cheap seats. Arthur Foods' warehouse is located nearby. Hot dogs, peanuts, popcorn, soda pop and the rest of the health food that makes the diet of the typical sportsfan leaves here to be distributed throughout the stadium. There was a steady stream of Arthur employees coming and going the entire time I spent in the warehouse. It was odd to be in there with all those boxes of peanuts and the sound of 30,000 fans filtering in through the open door. The game, taking place a few feet away, was on the radio.

Back outside, Dolly and Lisa were talking to Dodger usher Louis McDonald. The game was in a lull so they were just wandering around talking to people. It was a warm evening, and the Dodgers had the game in the bag. The aisles were full of fans whose attention and feet had wandered from the game. Some were eating, some talking, some just hanging out. This is an aspect of a game day at Dodger Stadium that rarely makes its way into the sports pages. It's a great place to meet people.

Annette Saldano notices people checking each other out from her food stand on the Field Level. "Yeah, one'll be on the first base side and the other on the third base side. They just ease slowly around and meet someplace in the middle. You notice it a lot more at day games when its warm, but it happens all the time."

Usher Marc Proval notices the same thing. "Hot August nights at the stadium. If the team's winning, and everybody's in a good mood, this place really jumps." Regrettably for Marc, the good spirits engendered by the warm weather also bring out the beach balls. Chasing them down is part of his job, but it is never fun.

Dolly Kejmar and Lisa Del Duca, 1988

RACHEL LOZZI, FROM BROOKLYN TO L.A.

After all those years, to have missed out on the celebration. To have cheered on the Dodgers through the slow years of World War II. To have watched her beloved team fall victim to the hated Yankees every time they did finally make it to the World Series. And then, after all this frustration, the Brooklyn Dodgers finally win the World Championship in 1955 – and Rachel Lozzi is in Italy.

Rachel clearly remembers the summer Sunday afternoons in the Dyker Heights section of Brooklyn where she grew up. Families inside, waiting for supper. Friends and relatives visiting. It was warm. Air conditioning in homes was still in the future, so windows were opened up and down 15th Avenue, making the air fragrant with the smell of pasta and sauce. Most of the homes and apartments had the radio on. Generally, to the Dodger game. As you walked down the street, you wouldn't miss a pitch. It wasn't that anyone was blasting their own radio. It was just that everyone was listening to the same thing.

Baseball seemed to surround Rachel when she was growing up. Neither of her Italian immigrant parents ever came to appreciate baseball, but her uncles and brothers loved it. Joe DePalma had one of the leading Cadillac dealerships in Brooklyn, and he and his niece would drive in style to Ebbets, parking on the street near the park, Joe often tossing a kid a dollar to make sure nothing happened to the car. Her other uncle, Nick D'Amario, had no children and loved to see the Dodgers. So he and Rachel would pile into his 1941 Pontiac and head for Flatbush to see their team. Nick would also find a place on the street to leave the car. Ebbets Field had space for only 350 cars.

In early 1955, Rachel went to Europe to study. The Dodgers got into the Series again, and, like always, she hoped for the best. The games were reported in Rome's English-language newspaper, *The American Observer*. She stayed up late to hear the Armed Forces Radio broadcasts from Germany to get more news of the Series. She had recently married, and no one in her new household spoke much English. Even if they had, "baseball was just this odd foreign thing to them." Besides, Rachel remembered, "they thought it was wrong for a woman to be so interested in some sport."

Rachel and her husband came to New York in 1957, but soon decided to move on. In November 1958, they drove to Southern California. "Everyone teased me that I came out here to follow the team." They settled in Orange County. She followed the Dodgers, but it wasn't the same anymore. She now had a family, and Garden Grove was so different. A typical postwar suburb. Lots of lawns and space, but no street life. She listened to the games, but in her own home.

Rachel thinks the team represented what was best about her hometown. "You know, Brooklyn was part of New York, but it seemed like a small town. The team had the spirit of a small town, it was something everyone could rally around. That's why your were so loyal to them. You thought of the Dodgers as your friends."

Rachel Lozzi, in the acres of parking lots, 1989

THE FANTASY LIFE

In 1973, Jack Lemmon won an Oscar for his portrayal of a businessman faced with the prospect of hiring an arsonist to burn down one of his buildings for the insurance money. The character grew up in Brooklyn, and as the pressure to pay for an illegal act to save his company grows, he finds momentary solace in trying to remember the starting line-up of the 1939 Dodgers. As the pressure continues to grow, he says to himself, "I shoulda been a ballplayer."

The active fantasy life of baseball fans is the reason Dodger Marketing and Promotions director Barry Stockhamer came up with the idea of "Think Blue Week." For years the team had received letters inquiring about the possibility of visiting areas of the stadium generally closed to fans. He thought: Why not give Dodger fans, "the truest of the Blue," an experience that money literally could not buy? So, for the past three seasons, during a week in mid-June just as schools are getting out for summer vacation, groups of Dodger supporters have had the chance to be a photographer, radio announcer, public address announcer, bat boy, groundskeeper, National Anthem singer, and usher.

Winning entries are chosen by Stockhamer and committees set up for each fantasy activity. The director has read several thousand of these letters over the past three years, and notes, "It's amazing how deeply entwined the Dodgers are in people's lives." Among Stockhamer's favorites are the two housewives who had not played together since being on their high school team. They got to take part in a softball game, played in Dodger uniforms at the stadium. "Walt the Ump," complete with his own business cards attesting to his calling, was the fantasy umpire. Another letter was from two former Little League teammates, now living at opposite ends of the country, who hoped to bat against Tommy Lasorda.

Their wish was granted, as was that of the young man who wanted to be a groundskeeper for the night and sweep the infield with the drag in the fifth inning. His mother wrote after the event, thanking the Dodgers for choosing her son, and expressing surprise at the kid's choice of fantasy. He never cleaned his own room and she was amazed that he was so keen to spiff up Dodger Stadium. But that is the point of fantasy. It takes us out of our lives to a place that no matter how mundane the work, is still an adventure.

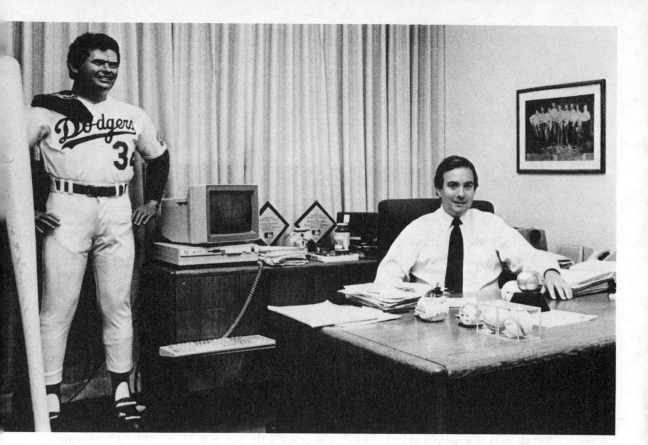

Barry Stockhamer, 1989

PEANUTS

The aim of a recent Planters Peanuts commercial was to tie the product in with both Americana and historical acceptance. What better way than to show a father and son enjoying a bag of warm peanuts fresh from the vendor's cart at an early-20th-century baseball game? The only other food as closely identified with the national pastime is the venerable hot dog.

There are dozens of peanut vendors sweating in the hot Los Angeles summer evenings as they hustle up and down aisles bringing their wares to Dodger fans. Warren Wald has been selling peanuts at the stadium ever since it opened in 1962. He is a man constantly in motion. "Peanuts! Peanuts, here!" he shouts as he runs. He will do this from pre-game until the eighth inning. Wald notes that peanut sales seem to be impervious to whether or not the team is winning. The two most important factors are fan location and the weather. The cheaper the seat and the lower the temperature, the faster he empties his vendor case.

It would figure that Los Angeles would be home to the most famous peanut vendor in the world. He is Roger Owens, "The Peanut Man." He is not only regularly cheered as he tosses the sacks behind his back, through his legs, and over his shoulder, he is often asked for his autograph. The man is a celebrity. Owens has tossed peanuts on *The Tonight Show*, *The Today Show*, and at President Jimmy Carter's inaugural party. Included in his press kit is a letter from L.A. Mayor Tom Bradley attesting to Owens' skill, talent as an entertainer, captivating personality, "and his excellent work as a Goodwill Ambassador for the City of Los Angeles."

This is pretty heady stuff. But whatever Owens has made of his talent once he discovered it, his start at the Coliseum in 1958 was strictly a matter of economic necessity. As the oldest of nine children, he had no choice but to go to work young when the family fortunes declined. As all food concessionaires do, he started out selling soda pop and ice cream. Peanuts is the best of the concessions because you can carry so many of them at once and because they are the only things that you can throw. Roger Owens has managed to make a career out of tossing bags of peanuts. One of the hallmarks of Los Angeles is that its lack of tradition has given people a chance to create themselves. Owens is a good example that it still does.

Roger Owens, "The Peanut Man," 1988

RICK FOREMAN ON A HOT DAY

Day game. A hot Sunday late in the summer. Rick Foreman is running through the concourse on the Field Level. He bursts through the door, headed for the Right Field Pavilion. A large case of frozen malts hangs from his shoulder. A distinct outline of sweat outlines the strap across his back. Rick is a big man and it helps. The case is full and it is not a light load.

Once in the pavilion, Foreman bounds up the steps leading to the seating area and immediately starts yelling, "Chocolate malts here! Get your ice cream here!" These are the most affordable seats in the stadium. Families are all over the place. It's also very hot. The malts move quickly. Up and down the rows. Stopping when hailed. Balancing the box on one leg. Passing out the malts, making change, and charging off to the next aisle. There is no hourly wage on this job. The hawkers are paid by a sliding percentage of their sales. Rick is a man constantly in motion.

The pavilions are Foreman's favorite place to work. There is less competition from other vendors and more families. He has seen many little kids grow into teenagers over the years, cheerfully eating his ice cream. Rick started working sports venues by selling the *Herald-Examiner* at the Coliseum. The newspaper used to print a special section that folded over the front of the regular paper and listed the teams playing that day and had several articles about the upcoming contest. For the Dodger games, it included a scorecard. He first got a job selling pennants when one of the vendor's crews failed to show up. He doesn't find much difference between sports when it comes to selling ice cream or soft drinks. But the weather definitely plays a part. Baseball works well for ice cream because it is "four months of heat." In cooler weather he generally switches to selling soda pop.

One of the most attractive things about working as a hawker for Arthur Foods is its part-time nature. In Rick's case this gives him more time to devote to Three Eye Productions. He and Robert Jones have set up talent shows and concerts all through the lively club scene in South Central Los Angeles. Their base of operations is the Dodger Club on Broadway. All the years of setting up shows have given Three Eye a huge backlog of performers to call upon when necessary. They are in the process of promoting a large concert starring bluesmaster Albert King and his band. All the supporting acts will be local talent, scouted and promoted by Rick and Robert Jones.

But for today, Foreman has sold his last malt. "Be right back," he tells the people grasping their dollars and looking longingly at the last malt as it is carried away through the heat and up the steps. Then he's gone. Pounding down the steps, bolting through the door, and running to get another box full of ice cream. There is still plenty of work to do before the ninth inning. Hard work on a hot day. But tonight Rick will be at the California Club on Martin Luther King Boulevard. There is a new singer he wants to see.

Rick Foreman, 1989

WORKING THE SCOREBOARD

If this was a book about a day in the life of Fenway Park in Boston instead of Dodger Stadium, some of the people I would have had to speak to would be the crew who worked inside the scoreboard in left field. Wrigley and Fenway are the only parks in the majors where scores are still hung by hand with metal numbers on hooks. At Dodger Stadium, if you want to know about the workings of the two large and two auxiliary scoreboards, you have to ask the Chief Electrician.

Bill Peebler has been following wire for the Dodgers for 25 seasons. He originally came to the stadium with the C.D. Draucker Company, which did the original wiring. Now he is out here all year round, making sure all the lights go on when a button is pushed. The off season is a time for general maintenance and completing any major changes. During the year, one of the chief concerns is making sure the scoreboards are working properly.

The main scoreboard in right field and the two auxiliary boards along the foul lines are operated from a master control located in front of Nancy Hefley's organ in the press box. They have been in place since the park opened in 1962. The board operator is responsible for watching the umpire signal whether the pitch is a ball or a strike, and punching the appropriate button to register the pitch on the scoreboard. He will listen to the official scorer, located just a few feet away in front of a microphone, for the determination if a questionable play was a hit or an error.

Peebler refers to the Diamond Vision board in left field as "basically just a big television set." True enough, but it is a real big TV 35 feet high and 75 feet long, in fact. To get inside, a technician has to first climb a spiral staircase, enter a trap door, then keep going up some more ladders once inside the board. Diamond Vision is the first such unit constructed by Mitsubishi in the United States. It replaced a large message board, and was unveiled at the 1980 All Star game held at the stadium. He notes that his job on the board is "mainly just lamp changing" – as well as fuses, breakers, and relays. But it takes a crew of six to operate the board during a game.

Mark Tamar is the director of the Diamond Vision team. They are packed into a small room next to the press box along with a television station full of equipment. In this compact space, there are a slow-motion machine, four VCRs, a tape deck, turntable for sound, graphics control, video image storage with team and individual images, a computer to keep track of the players' batting averages, and a teletype to stay in touch with action around the league. The director is also in charge of the Dodger video cameramen. Great plays can be shown on the screen seconds after they occurred. He also has the duty of directing the crew to zero in on one of the Dodgers who the team feels has developed some glitch in his swing or delivery.

Diamond Vision crew, 1989

NICK NICKSON

Nick Nickson was looking for a summer job. He is the color commentator on the KLAC broadcasts of the Kings' hockey games, so his winter months are busy ones. He has always been a baseball fan and has followed the Dodgers fortunes ever since moving to Los Angles from New Haven in 1981. The following year, he heard that longtime stadium announcer John Ramsey was retiring following the 1982 season. Nickson called the Dodgers to inquire after the job, went in for an audition, won the job and found himself sitting in the press box behind the stadium microphone at the start of the 1983 season. So he had his summer job.

Nickson likes the contrast between hockey and baseball. The winter sport is all motion and constant action. The summer game is more gradual in its buildup, with more intricate strategy. Since his primary duty is to announce each batter, Nickson has plenty of time to mull over the strategy that Tommy Lasorda might be hatching. The tranquility and mental exercise of the ball-park is the perfect break after the manic intensity of covering the Kings. Still, after the slower pace of baseball, he is looking forward to describing some more hockey. The two sports dovetail perfectly. The end of each season leaves him looking forward to the start of the other sport.

Nickson gets to Dodger Stadium two hours before game time. He will have dinner in the press dining room and go over the script for tonight's game. This is prepared by the Dodgers' group sales department and outlines any pre-game ceremonies scheduled for the day. After dinner, he will look up the opposition's broadcasters to make sure he has the pronunciation of the players' names correct. He will also ask them if there are any personnel changes on the visiting team.

This type of preparation pays off. Nickson has never had any glaring mistakes in his six seasons as Dodger public address announcer. The worst one he could think of occurred in his second game, when he looked down at his scorecard and announced that the catcher, "Steve" Scioscia, was coming to bat. It was the last time he wrote down only the last name of any player in his scorecard.

Nick Nickson, 1988

USHERS

Tyra Willis is on the Reserved Seat level. She will spend the night giving directions, making sure that no one was hurt by the rare foul ball that makes it up this high, talking to fans, and generally adding to the friendly ambience of Dodger Stadium. She is in her second season wearing the blue dress of the usherette, and hopes there will be several more. Tyra echoes the sentiment of most of the ballpark employees who are also fans. "It's like having a season ticket and getting paid for it."

Work at a baseball stadium is not only seasonal, it is also dependent on the team playing home games. The front-office people work all year long, as do the groundskeepers and gardeners. Not so the ushers, vendors, and cleanup crew. Tyra is generally found in the customer relations office of a Toyota dealership. Her manager is flexible about hours during the baseball season. As for Tyra, she not only likes seeing so many games, she also appreciates the way the game "breaks up the everyday routine of the office."

Marc Proval is one level lower in the Loge section. This is his fifth season with the Dodgers and he also is in no hurry to see his part-time job end. "Can you name me a better summer job for a baseball fan?" he asked. Like most of the other people I spoke with, he got the job because he knew someone who already worked at the stadium. His English teacher at Fairfax High School was an assistant operations director at the park. He told Marc he had to give him a C and not a B – as he had originally hoped. The good news was he had a summer job for him.

Even this most ideal of all jobs has its down side. Marc notes that sometimes fans will start to argue among themselves, and an attempt has to be made to get one of the verbal combatants to move. Intoxicated people remain a problem, but are fewer in number since the decision was made to serve beer in smaller cups and to stop pouring it altogether in the bottom of the seventh inning. Dodger security, or one of the various off-duty L.A.P.D. officers hired by the team for an emergency, handle any truly problematic fans.

This leaves the one thorn in the side of every usher. It is the only thing sure to draw the wrath of the fans on the usually well-received usher. Marc grew solemn. "I'm speaking, of course, of the dreaded beach ball. It is our duty to confiscate it and that never makes anyone happy."

Ushers, 1989

PART THREE: POST-GAME

Even in a close game, some fans start to leave after the seventh inning. After the last out, most of the people still in the stadium get up to go. But there are always those few bitter-enders. Whether they just want to soak up as much of the ambience of the ballpark as possible or just don't want to deal with the congestion sure to be found in the parking lot, they remain in their seats until the ushers move in to start clearing out the area. This sort of fan probably got to Dodger Stadium early to watch batting and infield practice. He or she will be visible in the parking lot playing catch or tossing a Frisbee. The more poetic will be in one of the lots above the Pasadena Freeway, savoring the best view in Los Angeles of the constantly evolving downtown skyline.

As soon as the last of the fans have moved away from their seats and started for their cars, an army of cleaning people descend on the vacated stadium. They will spend the night sweeping, hauling, hosing, and waxing until the ballpark is spotless and prepared for the next day's onslaught. While the cleanup crew is removing all the trash, Arthur Foods workers will be replenishing the concession stands. Elsewhere, stock people for Facility Merchandising, Inc., are preparing the vendor stands for tomorrow's game. Down on the field, the grounds crew is doing some minor maintenance on the field. They will return about noon to make sure the playing field is ready for a major league game.

Little of what happens late at night at Dodger Stadium has much drama. It is kin to batting and infield practice. It seems dull and repetitive on the surface, but without it the game would not flow smoothly. Lots of work is done once the game is over. Tons of trash are hauled out of Dodger Stadium after every home game. The dirt and grass of the playing surface has to be constantly tended or it will adversely effect the game. None of this tends to make the news. But all of it is vital to the operating of the ballpark.

The stadium, late, emptied

POST-GAME INTERVIEW, DUGOUT

The Dodgers just beat the Braves, 2–0, on a Mike Scioscia home run. As the stands empty and the parking lots fill, the catcher is sitting in the dugout speaking into a radio microphone. Don Drysdale, who now conducts the post-game interview for the English-language stations on the Dodger radio network, is sitting to the right of Scioscia. The initial questions will have to do with the home run. The others will deal with the catcher's tender heel and his thoughts about the upcoming National League Championship Series.

Two print journalists are also listening in on the conversation. They may ask a few questions in the dugout once the radio segment is closed, but most of their queries will take place back in the informality of the clubhouse. Television is also more likely to be away from the dugout. The strong lights necessary for video cameras leave harsh shadows behind the subject. They will normally be in the more brightly lit clubhouse or out on the field.

The man sitting to Scioscia's left is René Cardenas. He and Jaime Jarrin announce the Dodger games in Spanish. The flagship station for the Spanish-language broadcasts is KWKW in Los Angeles. Their signal is bounced off a satellite in order to beam the game to parts of Latin America. The Spanish-language network involves even more stations and reaches more people than its English counterpart.

KWKW uses the same format as KABC. Both feature pre- and post-game interviews. But as is the case with the other Spanish-language stations covering all of California's major league teams, KWKW's interviews have to be translated. Some of the Dodgers, such as Fernando Valenzuela or Alfredo Griffin, speak the language natively. Others, like Tommy Lasorda, Mike Scioscia, Steve Sax, and Franklin Stubbs, speak enough to get by. There is also Ron Perranoski, who knows eight or nine Spanish phrases and always manages to work them into the conversation. If the guest speaks no Spanish at all, the announcer will simply translate whatever is said. In the event that René Cardenas and Don Drysdale are set to speak to the same player after a game, Jaime Jarrin will give scores and recap the game until the English interview is completed. He will then introduce Cardenas and his guest, and they will be heard internationally.

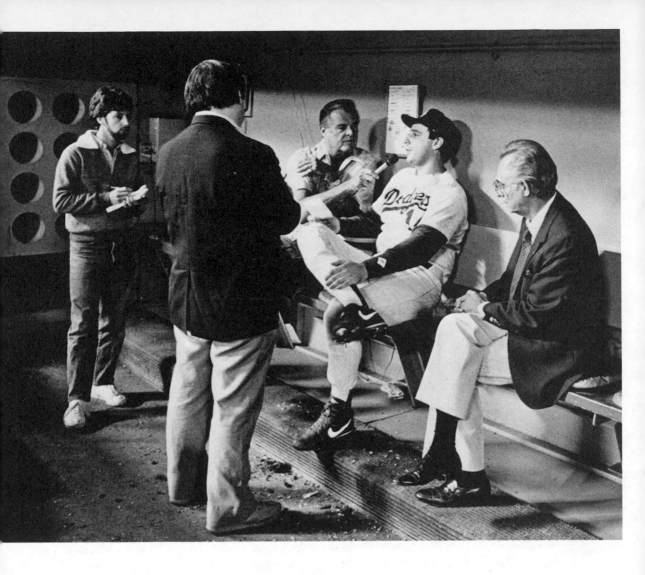

Mike Scioscia, dugout interview, 1988

POST-GAME, CLUBHOUSE

The clubhouse after a victory is cheerful chaos. Players are running about in various stages of undress, reporters are crowded around one or more lockers, bat boys are pushing huge carts filled with soiled uniforms toward the washing machine, and in the hall outside, the Dodgers' spikes are being washed in another machine. Tonight the pitching hero was Orel Hershiser and the winning run was knocked in by Mike Marshall. Both of them have reporters gathered around, especially Hershiser. There is even one intrepid woman reporter taking notes as Orel speaks. This is still a fairly rare sight in this most masculine of environments.

Kirk Gibson scored the winning run tonight. He has his share of reporters to deal with. The microphones are from radio reporters who will use them in later broadcasts. Television crews are usually present only late in the season and film often in the clubhouse. This privilege is denied still photographers, who lack official permission from the Dodger front office. Pictures are supposed to be taken only out in the hallway prior to entering the room. Transgressors are brought to the attention of Dave Wright, Dodger clubhouseman, who will explain the rules. The clubhouse gives players a chance to decorate their cubicle as they see fit. Kirk Gibson has a Michigan State pennant hanging from his. Orel Hershiser has pictures of his family tacked up. Fernando Valenzuela also has photos of his family, as well as a card of Our Lady of Guadalupe. Mickey Hatcher has a helmet with small bobbing baseballs attached by wire on a hook at his locker. Jeff Hamilton's just has his name and number.

Reportedly, it is the camaraderie of the locker room that former athletes generally miss the most once they have retired. It is easy to see why. Everyone – reporters, clubhousemen, bat boys – are subtly excluded here. There is nothing stated by the players and they are usually willing to cooperate so long as the rules are observed. But far more than the field at batting practice, this is their space, and anyone entering it who is not a player is an outsider.

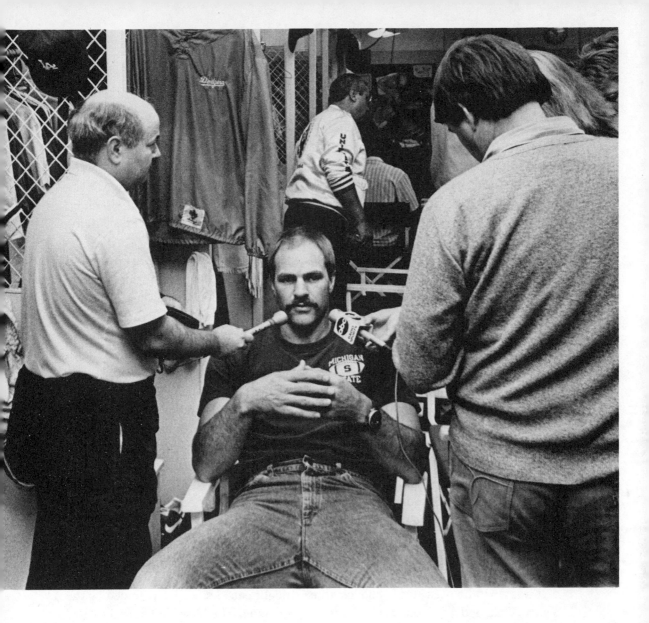

Kirk Gibson, clubhouse interview, 1988

A HISTORIC MEETING

The Dodgers were struggling in late August, but had certainly not given up hope. The pitching was still strong and Kal Daniels and Lenny Harris had recently arrived via a trade with the Reds to add some offensive sock. The Giants did not have a lock on the division. A few key wins and the team was convinced it could be right back in the race.

The Mets were coming to town. Their 1989 season had also been one of frustration. They were hoping to repeat as champions of the Eastern Division of the National League, but would have to catch the first-place Cubs. There was built-in drama to a Dodgers–Mets game in 1989. The previous October they had battled in the inclement New York weather to see who would represent the National League in the World Series. Though definite underdogs, the Dodgers had won. Ten months later, both teams were intent on getting back in their respective divisional races.

An added attraction to tonight's Dodgers–Mets game was the pitching match-up: Orel Hershiser versus Frank Viola. Not only were two of the premier hurlers in the game facing each other, it was the first time in baseball history that the previous year's Cy Young Award winners dueled each other in a regular season game. Los Angeles baseball fans responded in kind. There were 10,000 more people in the park than attended the previous night.

The game came off as advertised. A real pitcher's duel. Only one scratch run scored all night. Regretfully for the home team fans, it was scored when a single by Gregg Jefferies and a ground out by Juan Samuel combined with a another single by Howard Johnson to score a run for the Mets in the third inning. Viola kept the Dodgers to three hits to record his second win for the Mets.

It was a win he needed. He had lost three straight games since being traded by the Twins. Viola had a big contract and was not producing. The New York fans and press were not happy, and were quite vocal in their displeasure. He cheerfully talked to the press about the game and its historic dimension in his post-game interviews.

Orel Hershiser, on the other hand, was not a happy man. He is not a complainer nor a blamer. But tonight he was very frustrated. He pitched a wonderful game, scattering eight hits and allowing only one run before being replaced by Ray Searage in the ninth. As always, reporters converged on Hershiser's locker. The pitcher was very disappointed, as might be expected. "I've allowed six runs in my last 30 innings and I'm 0–2. That's all I can say." His was not the only pained face in the clubhouse. No professional likes to lose, but this one was particularly bitter. August 28 was a hard night for the Dodgers.

Frank Viola, post-game interview, 1989

TOMMY LASORDA
AND THE AMERICAN IDEAL

The American male ideal has traditionally involved strong, silent men who were self-contained loners bent stoically to a task. Gary Cooper, Humphrey Bogart, John Wayne, Clint Eastwood, and Sylvester Stallone have played the role often in the movies. Sizing up a problem, meeting it head-on, solving it with as few words as possible, moving on without thanks when the task was done. Funny, gregarious, witty men sometimes appeared as sidekicks or comic relief. But they were never in charge, and rarely to be taken seriously.

This is Tommy Lasorda's problem. Since replacing Walter Alston as Dodger manager in 1977, Lasorda has a .593 winning percentage. His teams have won six Western Division titles, four National League pennants, and two World Championships. In 1988 he was voted Manager of the Year for his role in helping lead the Dodgers to a pennant after two consecutive fifth-place finishes. All this success and still it seems hard to take him seriously. Lasorda with his emotionalism, bombast, and outrageous good humor simply does not fit the Pattonesque stereotype of a sports leader.

To an unusual degree, Lasorda's office reflects the man within. Walter Alston worked out of an unadorned, small space now used as the coaches office. When Lasorda took the job, he moved to a larger room and immediately started decorating. There is a uniform locker, of course, with a few trophies on it, and a big-screen television. The walls are completely covered with photographs and drawings. Both Frank Sinatra and Don Rickles have their own exhibits. The rest of the space is devoted to ballplayers active and retired, family pictures, and religious messages.

Win or lose, the door is open after a game. A table groans with the post-game meal. Players wander in and out. Newsmen question the manager about the team's performance. The phone rings constantly. Lasorda presides over the proceedings, answering questions, cajoling players, telling jokes and baseball stories. Always talking a mile a minute. Loose, enjoying himself. Not acting anything remotely like John Wayne or Vince Lombardi. Seeming to be every inch the comic-relief sidekick, not the main star. But he knows baseball, and his teams win. Why should he be faulted for having so much talent for telling a story?

Tommy Lasorda in his office, 1988

ONSTAGE AND BACKSTAGE
WITH THE BAT BOYS

My great-uncle, John Connor, was a bat boy for the Chicago White Sox and later an umpire in the Class A California League. My childhood was filled with stories of the aggression of Ty Cobb, the kindness of Walter Johnson, the dominance of Babe Ruth, and the tragedy of "Shoeless Joe" Jackson. Fifty years after the fact, he remembered which kind of tobacco the different players would send him to pick up. Sometime in the mid-2030s Shawn Evans and Pete Sandoval will be sitting with their grand children, spinning yarns about the 1988 Dodgers, and their unlikely World Championship.

They are two of the six Dodger bat boys. The word is something of a misnomer. Both are men in their early twenties who started working for the Dodgers after playing ball at Pasadena City College. Their direct boss is Nobe Kawano, who has run the Dodger clubhouse ever since the team came west. The day's schedule will call for two men to work in the dugout, two on the foul lines, and two more back in the clubhouse.

Evans prefers the dugout post. Not only are you running around a bit – taking balls to the umpires and getting the bats – but you have a chance to listen to the talk on the bench and get a better insight into the strategy of the game. Working the foul lines is the second-best assignment. Here you will play catch with one of the outfielders, shag stray balls, and talk to fans. There can be long pauses between action, however, and April and September nights can be pretty cold at the stadium.

The night I talked to Pete Sandoval, he had the clubhouse duty. When I walked in right after the game, he already had the first post-game wash going. This is definitely the bat boy's backstage activity. He is responsible for making sure all the ballplayers' paraphernalia is collected and popped into the huge washing machine just outside the clubhouse. Persistent stains, such as those caused by sliding on grass, will be taken to Ophelia Grajeda, who works on them until they are gone.

Since players wear one uniform for batting practice and a second for the game, the washing machine has been turning most of the time the Dodgers spent beating the Braves. Pete will be here for another hour. He is up to his elbows in soiled uniforms and undershirts, with more arriving all the time. But no complaints. This is what it takes to be part of the show.

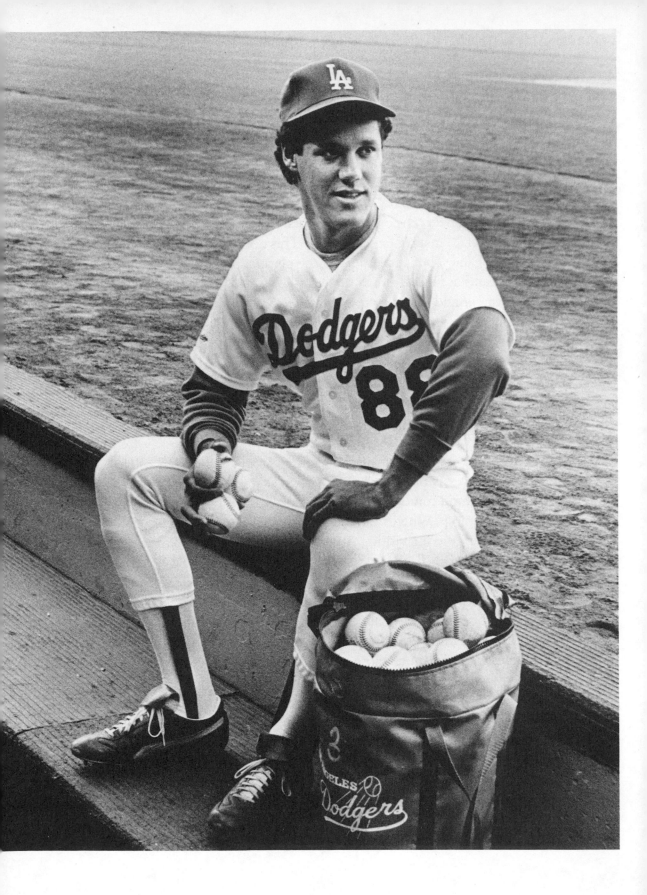

Shawn Evans, 1988

THE BUS DRIVERS

Bus drivers Ralph Garcia and Harry Carpenter see a lot of games but never pay for a seat. They are the drivers of the huge Grey Line buses that transport the visiting team players back and forth between their hotel and the ballpark. Garcia has driven for the company for years, but sees this as the best assignment he's had so far. "I'm a big fan," he says. "This not only gives me the chance to see a lot of games, but I meet lots of the players, too." The only drawback is that the teams are usually lousy tippers.

Both Garcia and Harry Carpenter note that much of their schedule is in the hands of the visiting team's traveling secretary. He will pick which of the downtown hotels the club will use – generally the Biltmore, Hyatt Regency, or Sheraton Grande – and what time the team will leave for Dodger Stadium. The chief variable in departure time from the hotel is whether or not the visitors are going to take batting practice. There is only one bus used on these runs unless it is getaway day. Then a second coach will be used to store all the added luggage and equipment. The extra space also helps if the team has lost. Often players will want to be as far away from the managers and coaches as possible.

While a driver is up on the Reserve Level watching the game, his bus is parked out behind center field. He starts making his way back to work during the eighth inning. When the Dodgers go on the road, Garcia or Carpenter are down south driving visiting American League teams to play the Angels at Anaheim Stadium. But being a Dodger fan of long standing, Ralph prefers working with the National League. So far, the Expos, Braves, and Pirates have been the most fun to be around. Any trip is improved, of course, if the team has won. Then it will leave about an hour after the last out, and be loose and joking in the manner of young men everywhere. After a loss, the team is out of the dressing room much more quickly and in a somber mood.

The only other problem Garcia and Carpenter have to deal with is the irrefutable law of nature that buses are never, under any circumstances, to sully the outfield grass. Maneuvering one of those behemoths through the center-field gate and around the foul line curves is no easy task. Sensing the obvious question, Garcia holds up his hands and says, "With practice, I'm getting better."

Harry Carpenter, 1989

VISITORS

Major league ballplayers spend half their season on the road. Los Angeles is just one more stop along the way for most. The only thing that sets it apart for some of them is the fact that it is their hometown.

Eddie Murray is an Angeleno by birth. He was not sure what it would be like to play in front of old schoolmates and neighborhood friends. It turned out well for the ex-Oriole. The transition was easier than he thought. Eric Davis of the Reds only comes to his hometown for nine games a year. Like Murray, he has also enjoyed playing in front of old friends. His family is the only lure he feels for coming back to Los Angeles to play baseball.

Davis' friend, Darryl Strawberry, was more open about his enjoyment of returning to his hometown. It gives him some time to visit with the family he sees so rarely during the long season. He did not see that many games at Dodger Stadium as a kid, preferring to see the Lakers at the Forum. But he clearly remembers playing for the city baseball championship for Crenshaw High School at the stadium. What was so different about playing that game was the lack of fans. "There were no people here. It was so quiet." Not so when Strawberry comes to bat for the Mets. He gets some of the loudest cheers for any visiting player.

Gary Carter is another hometown product. He was a big Dodger fan as a kid and saw lots of games at the stadium. Often at night, while falling asleep, he would imagine himself playing at what he calls "the Disneyland of parks." Carter is a man who is still very much in touch with the dreams of his childhood self. The catcher may be a dreamer, but he is also a realist. He wishes he could have played his entire career on the natural grass surface of Dodger or Shea Stadium. He is convinced the hard artificial surface in Montreal led to the leg problems that have shortened his career. "Turf hurts," he notes.

To the visiting players not native to the city, Los Angeles is just another stop on a road trip. Ken Griffey of the Reds used to like bringing his family along to L.A. on road trips "when the kids were young," because they enjoyed the various amusement parks so much. Astros outfielder Glenn Wilson has not found anywhere special to eat out here. His favorite places for eating on the road is Rusty's Ribs in New York and Ron of Japan in Chicago. With no one here to visit, Los Angeles is just another road city.

Braves visitor Dale Murphy, Tommy Lasorda, and Ken Gurnick, 1988

THE GIANTS' CLINCH

Tim Belcher pitched a masterful game, winning 1–0 for his league-leading eighth shutout. The Giants' magic number was down to one. All it would take for them to clinch the National League Western Division pennant was their own win or a loss by the Padres. But the Dodgers refused to help. Reporters surrounded the winning pitcher in the Dodger dugout to hear Don Drysdale's post-game interview, but soon scurried over to the Giants locker room to hear the outcome of the Padres–Reds game being played 125 miles to the south. There was no reason to rush. The game went into extra innings.

The Giants were hanging around in their underwear munching ice cream bars and trying to get reports from San Diego. Newsfolk stood around with plastic over their cameras wondering if they were going to have to follow the team south to see them finally win this thing. There was no one to talk to and little else to do but mill, which the combined press did in unison.

A radio link with San Diego was eventually set up in one of the back rooms of the clubhouse and most of the players went back to listen to the game. Periodic shouts emerged down the corridor as the Reds threatened in the eleventh, only to strand the runner.

There was obviously something brewing in the twelfth. Murmurs from the back room were followed by a raucous cheer, while visiting clubhouse manager Jim Muhe started pulling down plastic covers over the players' lockers. Sure enough, within minutes a boisterous shouting preceded the players running out of the back room into the main locker area. They were, of course, amply armed with champagne bottles, and began soaking everything and everyone in sight. The shower was accompanied by much hugging, laughing, and general good cheer. The Giants won the division, and if they could get past the Eastern Division champs, the Chicago Cubs, they would go to the World Series for the first time since 1962.

The special hats and tee-shirts with their Western Division champs logo were soon soaked. No one cared, of course. This is what these men had worked for all season. They were allowed to cavort and yell while the press recorded it all. It is rare that a man is allowed to act the part of a boy and not be chastised. In this case it is expected and encouraged. Tradition, even.

Will Clark, victory celebration, 1989

POST-GAME SECURITY

Post-game provisions for protection of the field differ from league city to league city. In New York's Shea Stadium, ushers ring the seats on the playing field to make sure that fans don't charge out on the diamond. This does not seem necessary at Dodger Stadium. Security will eventually try to hurry along the stragglers who remain in their seats rather than face the traffic in the parking lot. But, as always, they are very low key when there is no altercation to bring out a show of force. Once the fans have filed out, a few of the officers will check out the small group of fans waiting in the seats above the visitors' dugout to make sure they legitimately know one of the players and are not just hanging around for an autograph.

Elizabeth McClure is in her second season in Dodger Security. She is one of the 80 or so officers walking around the stadium during a game making sure nothing gets out of hand. She worked in security before coming to the Dodgers, and likes the mellow attitude of most of the fans at the ballpark. Like most everyone who works at the stadium, Liz has another job. She is the assistant track and cross-country coach at San Pedro's Banning High School.

Several other baseball fans have ideal part-time jobs as Dodger security officers. Larry Bloom is a student at Cal State Northridge and runs his own auto detailing business. Dan Solorza is one of the senior personnel with nine seasons on the job. He works for a personal injury law firm when he is not at the stadium. While they are working at their full-time jobs during the winter, there will still be a staff of security people protecting the stadium. As Solorza points out, it is private property. "And, you know, people are crazy about this place. Everytime when fans have been allowed on the field, I'll always see a couple of 'em reach down and grab some dirt or grass to take home for a souvenir."

The players slowly emerge from the clubhouse by way of the dugout. Most just climb on the bus. But those with waiting friends or families head up into the stands. Some visit for a while and walk down to the bus, some leave with the people who have been waiting for them. It is not a time of snapshots and autographs. It's just some guys getting a chance to spend some time with people they know in a city they are just visiting. Soon the stands are empty and the bus leaves. The cleaning crew moves in with the brooms.

Officer Elizabeth McClure, 1989

GROUNDS CREW

As soon as the last out is recorded the grounds crew goes back to work. The only time they are seen during a game is when the infield is dragged at the top of the fifth inning or if rain necessitates unrolling the tarp. But they are around the park nonetheless. It makes for a long day. The keepers of the field have been at work since before noon.

Al Hicks is fairly new to the Chavez Ravine. Prior to his Los Angeles arrival he worked for the Parks Department at Port Charlotte, Florida, with the Texas Rangers, and at the Dodgers facility, Vero Beach. He is as happy to be with the big club as Ramon Martinez. Hicks has served his apprenticeship in "sports facilities management." He notes that it is a specialized type of gardening and consists of "a little more than cuttin' the grass and rakin' the dirt."

Tonight, in the dimness of only half the stadium's lights, Hicks, Al Myers, Rico Rivera, and Vince Vasquez will only cover the batter's boxes and mound with small tarps and lightly water down the field. The real work comes tomorrow, but the sprinkling is important both to keep the playing field green and make sure the plate and mound keep their proper consistency. Hicks points out that hitters hate a soft batter's box. They want to be able to dig in. Likewise, if the mound is too soft the pitchers will dig holes all over it with their spikes, since their individual strides can be so different.

The morning will be the time to take the measurements. The outfield grass is cut every day and kept at $\frac{5}{8}$ of an inch. The infield is cut every other day, getting no longer than half an inch. Hicks notes that these lengths can change quite a bit around the league. Teams with slower fielders tend to keep the grass a bit longer to increase drag on the ball and thereby give the glovemen a split second longer to reach a groundball.

A nail drag is used to rip the top half-inch of the clay surface of the infield. If this were not done on a daily basis the top of the infield would bake as hard as a brick. Each day one and a half to two hours are spent on the preparation of the infield. The pitcher's mound takes special attention, also. The rubber cannot be higher than ten inches above the plate and the slope of the mound cannot be more than one inch per foot. Once all this work is done, the field is ready for major league baseball.

Rico Rivera wetting down home plate, 1988

THE SOUVENIR STAND

It's well over an hour since the conclusion of the game. The Dodgers lost to San Diego tonight, 5–4. Few fans stuck around to try and get an autograph after the bitter loss. Business was not much better at the souvenir stands. Hard losses and extra-innings games are awful for the vendors. Their best nights take place after a late-inning Dodger victory. Then everyone wants to take something home.

But win or lose, inventory goes on. So, while food supply trams rumbled by, Ray Kaulig counted pennants, caps, tee-shirts, and yearbooks. Also on the list was an item new this year: umpire cards. Full-color cards featuring the 31 National League umpires with a $15.00 price tag. The cards were printed by Paul Runge. Proceeds from sales went into a special fund for the umpires. Kaulig noted that the cards sold fairly well for so expensive an item.

Many of the vendor's items are perennials and sell pretty evenly throughout the season. Caps are an example of this, or pennants. Team logo jackets sell better in cold weather, while tee-shirts sell better when it's warm. Yearbooks, as you would expect, sell more quickly at the beginning of the year. Everything sells better when the team is winning, but the percentage of people buying small bats, dolls, or wristbands doesn't seem to change that drastically. A customer in the market for more esoteric items – such as books about the Dodgers or broken bats used by team members – will have to forsake the local souvenir stand for the Dodger Gift Shop. It is open all year long and located on the Top Deck.

The one drawback to a job at the stadium for a dedicated baseball fan is summed up in Kaulig's comment that he has been to every Dodger game for the past five years but hasn't seen one of them. It drives David Taliaferro nuts to hear the distinct roar of a crowd excited by a play or hit as he is making his hot dogs in Annette Saldano's concession stand on Field Level. Sometimes when he gets a bit ahead in his hot dog cooking, he takes a moment to run out and see what is happening on the field. Marc Proval thinks this is why being an usher is one of the best jobs in the stadium. He is almost always in a position to keep one eye on the action. For the same reason, Shawn Evans would rather spend his evening bat-boying from the dugout rather than washing clothes back in the clubhouse. Most of those working at the stadium are there because it is a good way to make some extra money while indulging their interest in baseball.

Ray Kaulig doing inventory, 1988

THE CLEANUP CREW

No sooner has Dodger security made sure the last of the fans are moving toward the exits than an army of cleaners descends on the seats. Various parts of the force will work most of the night. When they leave, Dodger Stadium, the third-oldest ballpark in the National League, will look brand new.

The "sweepers" are the first of the crews to get to work. You can hear them all over the empty stadium as they pop up the seat bottoms with their brooms to get at the refuse underneath. Adeline Tamez is a supervisor with the sweepers and notes that she generally has about 40 people in her crew. More are brought in when the crowd is larger. During the game they have been sweeping up in the public walkways and making sure the restrooms stay clean. At its conclusion they will push all the trash discarded under the seats into the center aisles. The shovel crew moves in at this point to lift the trash into small containers, and eventually to empty these into the larger dumpsters located in the walkways.

Once the sweepers and shovelers have cleared out the trash, the hose team comes in to spray down the seats and aisles. Tonight Samuel Saldana will wash the entire Orange Level with a high-powered hose. Meanwhile, the "mop men" are cleaning the concourse areas in preparation for the arrival of the "deck men" in their tractorized waxing units.

As the cleaning crews go about their business, beer and food trains are making their rounds taking perishables to the Arthur Foods storage space on the Blue Level and replacing needed non-perishables. Tomorrow, fresh hot dogs and peanuts will arrive at the stands. Beer kegs and soda pop syrup containers will be connected and ready to serve thirsty fans.

After every home game it's the same thing. Men and women with brooms, hoses, and shovels remove tons of trash while other workers mop, wax, fill up the food stands, and sweep the parking lots. By the time the first fans start to filter into the park at 6:00 p.m., the place will be so clean it is impossible to tell there was an event held in the stadium the previous day.

Carlos René de Leon sweeping Field Level, 1989

GETAWAY DAY

It's early June and the Dodgers have just split a four-game series with the second-place Houston Astros. The Dodgers won today. Orel Hershiser beat the all-time strikeout leader in baseball history, Nolan Ryan. The clubhouse is loose. Kirk Gibson has an ice pack on his right knee. He is telling a group of reporters that they should quit worrying so much about all the guys on the Disabled List. "You can't worry about that. We raise each other up. That's what being a team's all about."

Orel Hershiser is at his locker, surrounded by reporters. The right sleeve has been entirely cut off the gray tee-shirt he wears under his long-sleeved undershirt. A sweat stain extends all the way down the right side of the shirt. He answers questions from the assembled scribes and accepts congratulations from teammates with the same serious demeanor. When the last reporter has asked his questions, Hershiser asks respectfully, "Is that enough?" He finally can take his shower.

Lasorda is holding court in his office. The television is on, the table loaded with food, the reporters ready with their notebooks in hand. The manager looks up to see Steve Sax walk in the office to discover what's to eat. "Hey, Saxy," he yells, "look who's on TV." Sax moves over to where he can see the giant screen. He pauses to watch the Three Stooges awhile. "I love these guys," he says.

Meanwhile, back in the tunnels under the stands the equipment trucks are being loaded. This is a getaway day. Tomorrow night the Dodgers will play the Padres in San Diego. Bats, balls, gloves, uniforms, and hats have to be loaded into bags, carted out to the waiting truck, and driven south down Interstate 5. If the team were headed east, all the equipment would be driven to the airport. Jim Barnhart and his crew will load 4,800 pounds' worth of Dodger gear this night. And that doesn't even include the luggage each team member will carry with him. Barnhart figures to drive as far as San Onofre. He will stop there and eat some dinner while watching the Laker game before pressing on to San Diego. By 3:30 tomorrow, when the players start to arrive at the visitors' clubhouse at Jack Murphy Stadium, they will find their uniforms and equipment laid out and waiting for them. But that's tomorrow. Tonight the truck is still to be loaded.

Jim Barnhart and crew, 1988

THE PLAYERS' PARKING LOT

The Dodger team parking lot is reached by walking down a long corridor past the weight room, shower room, and batting cage and then climbing the stairs to a gate located just behind the home team bullpen. Inside the lot, the player will find both his car and several guards. Ringing the chain link fence, and often hanging over it, he will be confronted by fans calling for him to come over and give them an autograph.

The autograph seekers are predominantly male and young. They are noisy and demanding when a player appears, but rarely surly. The kids, of course, are the most energetic. They are the ones precariously hanging over the top of the fence loudly begging whichever Dodger is in the lot to come over and give them a signature. The player will be escorted to his car by one or more of the L.A.P.D. or Dodger officers. Whatever abuse comes the player's way is only verbal, and usually not vicious. Gary Hinderaker considers this duty a vacation after some of the problems he has to deal with on his police beat. "At least here we're dealing with decent people."

If the player decides to sign some autographs, he usually does so near his car. Styles of signing differ markedly. Steve Sax signs for a short time each day. When the time he has set for himself is up, he says, "Gotta go," hops in his car and is gone. Rick Dempsey, reaching the end of his career, and Jeff Hamilton, at the beginning of his, generally ride home together. They sign almost every night, as do Franklin Stubbs and Mike Scioscia. They are only rarely joined by Jesse Orosco and Mike Marshall. Kirk Gibson prefers to answer autograph requests through the mail he receives at the stadium.

Don Sutton, a 300-game-winning pitcher in the last months of his career, did not mind signing autographs in the least. When asked if he had any idea how many times he had signed something for someone, he said, "No idea. I just keep hoping I get to do it one more time."

John Shelby will usually give some autographs. He sees it as part of the game, but notes that the fans in L.A. are a lot more dedicated to getting a signature than the ones he left behind when he was traded from the Baltimore Orioles. "They will be out there in the rain or after an extra-inning game. Anytime. People in Baltimore wanted to go home." It seems fitting that in the film capital of the world the autograph seekers would not only be more numerous but also more persistent.

John Shelby autographing in the player's parking lot, 1988

THE OBJECT OF THEIR DESIRE

America in the late 20th century is a nation with few heroes but many idols. Never has the craze for securing the signature of famous people been more manic. Events such as book signings, personal appearances, and premieres are designed to give the public a chance to play a peripheral but immediate part in the lives of the object of their desire. This type of idol worship is hardly unique to the United States, but the open nature of our society and the demands of its democratic myths of equality make Americans particularly insistent on having access to the stars.

Baseball players are the most popular sports figures when it comes to autographs. One of the latest wrinkles in the exploding market for baseball cards is the appearance of both retired and current ballplayers at card conventions. A Mickey Mantle autograph might cost a fan $30 while Wade Boggs signs for $15. At that, the lines are usually long.

Autographs at Dodger Stadium don't cost anything. You will see players writing their names on pictures, cards, and balls as they wait for batting practice or the game to start. Some will sign for fans along the third base line during pre-game warm-ups. Most take a moment at least to work the crowded fence in the players' parking lot after the game. This is usually done doggedly, with an absolute minimum of conversation. Dodgers will usually answer any question directed at them as briefly as possible. There always seems to be someone in any collection of fans who is so lost in the bitterness of his own lack of fulfillment that he can't help but express anger at the favored individual being asked for an autograph. The players have all experienced this a hundred times before. They protect themselves by being cordial, but not friendly. There is always something held in reserve when they are in a crowd of fans.

Whenever it seems the player is about to leave, the plea for "just one more" inevitably starts. "How come you never understand when a guy's got someplace to be?" asked John Shelby. Not really a question. No answer was offered.

But leave they must. "Gotta go," says Steve Sax. "My family is waiting for me," says John Shelby. Usually the fans will shout their thanks when it is apparent that the player will sign no more that night. But occasionally you will get a plaintive cry like the one that followed Kirk Gibson into his car one night. A man stood against the fence and wailed over and over, "Kirk, man, you just don't understand!"

No doubt he doesn't.

Orel Hershiser IV and (lower left) V, 1988

ENDGAME

It's late at night. The players' parking lot is empty, the policemen guarding it have all gone home. Only a few fans were looking for signatures tonight. The Dodgers suffered a tough 5–4 loss to the Padres on an eighth-inning home run that probably should have been caught. There was plenty of room around the fence, for once. It must have been evident to everyone that tonight was the wrong time to ask for an autograph. Most of the players just walked through the gate leading to the lot and headed directly to their cars, heads down. Very few shouts of "Kirk, Kirk!" or "Steve, Steve!" tonight. About the only ones to do any signing were Rick Dempsey and Jeff Hamilton. Everyone knows it is just a matter of time until the Dodgers clinch the Western Division title. Tonight did not bring it any closer to home.

Tommy Lasorda was subdued, also. He takes it for granted his team will clinch soon, but this is a man who hates to lose. As always his office is full of people. The gloom of the past two losing seasons is nowhere in evidence, but neither is the ebullience that follows a victory. Lasorda is telling a reporter from Japan that the 1988 Dodgers are better than the past two years because the gaping holes that have plagued the team were filled during the off season. The manager credits Dodger Vice President Fred Claire for going out and getting the right players to plug the gaps, and President Peter O'Malley for giving him both the go-ahead and the funding to get quality players.

The acres of asphalt that surround the stadium are empty. The fans, players, and vendors have all gone home. The ballpark is only dimly lit as the cleaning crews go about their nocturnal rounds. The only sounds in the Ravine are the metallic clanking of the beer trains and the whining of the air blowers used to clean the stands. An occasional shout from one of the workers is audible. Otherwise all is silence. It is like seeing "Old Ironsides," the U.S.S. *Constitution*, tied up in Boston Harbor. The sight is beautiful but seems unnatural. Ships should be at sea and ballparks should be full of fans excited by the spectacle before them. At least the freeways aren't crowed this early in the morning. They look great empty.

Dodger coaches, 1988

AFTERWORD:
"DODGER DAY DOWNTOWN"—
THE VICTORY PARADE

One of the primary attractions of professional sports is their appeal to the thirst for grandeur in people's lives. There is little risk to the fan in the rocky quest for greatness. It is perfectly safe to invest your emotions in a team because the triumphs or failures are all vicarious. Whether your team wins or loses, you will still have the same job, same relationships, same debts.

But even vicarious thrills can be sublime. On October 24, 1988, the World Champion Los Angeles Dodgers were fêted with a celebration organized by the city and called "Dodger Day Downtown." The team was cheered down Broadway as they rode on a series of floats. The destination was the steps of City Hall, where the main rally was to take place. In all, over 70,000 people took the chance to share in the Dodgers' triumph.

As adulation rained down on the team over on Broadway, the crowd at City Hall was entertained with a tape of Vin Scully's World Series calls. "Glory Days" and "Center Field" were played over the sound system. When the floats bearing the players pulled up on the Main Street side of City Hall, "I Love L.A." blasted out of the loudspeakers. As the Dodgers were working their way to the place of honor, six helicopters circled overhead to record the event for the evening news. Down on the ground, the fans yelled, banners were unfurled, signs lifted high. The crowd reveled in its chance to be a direct participant in celebrating the team's gritty triumph over the Oakland Athletics.

The Stuntmen and the stars all had their time in the sun. Kirk Gibson, Mickey Hatcher, Steve Sax, and the fan's obvious favorite, Orel Hershiser, all spoke briefly to the crowd. Vin Scully narrated the event, Mayor Tom Bradley welcomed everyone, the U.C.L.A. cheerleaders frolicked, the Dodger wives were cheered, Tommy Lasorda danced, and the attending politicians had the good sense to just sit and share in the reflected glory.

The disappointing 1986 and 1987 seasons proved conclusively that all the Dodgers have to do is put nine men in blue-and-white uniforms on the field to draw two million people. The city loves their team. Uncomplicatedly and unequivocally. Fans will show up to see a poor team in great enough numbers, but give them a year-long contender and almost three million people will show up at the stadium.

Given a World Championship to celebrate, 70,000 of those fans happily and non-violently crowded downtown to express their joy in the Dodgers' triumph — and to share in the grandeur.

Tommy Lasorda at "Dodger Day Downtown," 1988

DODGER STADIUM:
A PHOTO ESSAY

My earliest memories of baseball involve a dirt lot with a high fence in West-chester, Steve Bilko hitting for the Angels while the legend "56 home runs" flashed on the TV screen—and the Topps 1957 baseball card set. That was the year my friend Mark Michelson and I both started trying to hit a baseball and to collect cards. My favorite player was Mickey Mantle but my favorite team was the Dodgers. The pictures on the cards all showed this odd stadium in the background behind the players, who were decked out in the neatest blue-and-white uniforms.

Like all eight-year-old Angeleno baseball fans, I was ecstatic when the Dodgers moved west. I usually listened to most of the games on a white plastic radio, sometimes keeping score. But bunches of the neighborhood kids were often taken to the game by someone's parents, and even as kids we knew that the Coliseum was a football or track-and-field venue. It was an awful place to see a baseball game. All of us were anxious to see the new park in Chavez Ravine.

I was twelve when my father took me to a St. Louis Cardinal game soon after Dodger Stadium opened in 1962. Bob Gibson was pitching that night. We were not the only people in the city to want to see him work. You could always get into the Coliseum. It had space for 93,000 fans. Dodger Stadium seated 56,000, and this night, it was sold out. We first tried the reserved seats. No luck. So, we slid down the bare dirt that led from one parking lot to the next to see if there was any space left in the pavilions. Nope. So my father took me to see Mickey Mantle and Roger Maris in one of the hokier baseball movies of all time, *Safe at Home*.

Those dirt hills are long gone. One of the best things about Los Angeles is that almost anything will grow here. Very little of what is planted today is native to the place. But then, neither is the water that makes it flower. L.A. is the ultimate man-made city. The harbor is dredged, the river is diverted. But our landscaping is an eclectic delight.

Dodger Stadium is a beneficiary of this. Gentle, rolling hills surround the parking lots. Lush gardens welcome you to the stadium proper, while inside there is a huge expense of thick, green grass. Like most large structures, it is most interesting when viewed in its parts. There are all sorts of interesting angles and dramatic light effects in the park. It is worth a close look.

A LOS ANGELES BASEBALL BIBLIOGRAPHY

The best source for following baseball in Los Angeles is the daily sports pages of the various local newspapers. The Pacific Coast League was closely covered in the now-defunct *Daily News* (whose "morgue" is available at the U.C.L.A. Research Library) and *Hollywood Citizen News*, as well as in the *Los Angeles Times*, *Herald*, and *Examiner*.

GENERAL

Henstell, Bruce, *Sunshine and Wealth: Los Angeles in the Twenties and Thirties* (San Francisco: Chronicle Books, 1984).

Reidenbaugh, Lowell, *Take Me Out to the Ballpark* (St. Louis: Sporting News, 1983).

Torrence, Bruce T., *Hollywood: The First Hundred Years* (New York: New York Zoetrope, 1982).

Weaver, John D., *Los Angeles: The Enormous Village, 1781–1981* (Santa Barbara: Capra Press, 1980).

PACIFIC COAST LEAGUE

Beverage, Richard, *The Angels: Los Angeles in the Pacific Coast League* (Placentia, Calif.: Deacon Press, 1981).

————, *Hollywood Stars: Baseball in Movieland, 1926–1957* (Placentia, Calif.: Deacon Press, 1984).

Goodale, George, *The Los Angeles Angels Baseball Club and All-Time Record Book* (Los Angeles: Los Angeles Angels Baseball Club, 1951).

Lange, Fred, *History of Baseball in California and Pacific Coast Leagues, 1847–1938* (Oakland: Lange, 1938).

Panella, Bob, "All Eras End – And With Memories," *Hollywood Citizen-News*, March 3, 1958, p. 12.

Professional Baseball Parks in the Los Angeles Area (Los Angeles: City of Los Angeles Bicentennial Project, 1981).

Rowe, David G., *Pacific Coast Baseball League Records, 1903–1954* (San Francisco: Pacific Coast Baseball League, 1955).

Schroeder, W. R., *The Pacific Coast League from 1903 to 1940* (Los Angeles: Helms Athletic Foundation, 1941).

Spink, J. G. Taylor, "Cobb Flings Coast All-Star Challenge," *The Sporting News*, January 14, 1948, p. 5.

Zimmerman, Tom, "Before Dodger Stadium," *Dodger Scorecard Magazine*, July 1987, pp. 20–21.

LOS ANGELES DODGERS

Finch, Frank, *The Los Angeles Dodgers: The First Twenty Years* (Virginia Beach: Jordan & Co., 1977).

Henderson, Cary S., "Los Angeles and the Dodger War, 1957–1962," *Southern California Quarterly*, Vol. 62 (Fall 1980), pp. 261–89.

Hines, Thomas S., "Housing, Baseball, and Creeping Socialism: The Battle of Chavez Ravine, Los Angeles, 1949–1959," *Journal of Urban History*, Vol. 8 (February 1982), pp. 123–43.

Los Angeles Dodgers, *Media Guide* (Los Angeles: Dodgers, printed annually since 1958).

Poulson, Norris, *Memoirs*, oral history project (University of California at Los Angeles: Special Collections).

Sullivan, Neil J., *The Dodgers Move West* (New York: Oxford University Press, 1987).

Wood, Bob, *Dodger Dogs to Fenway Franks: The Ultimate Guide to America's Top Baseball Parks* (New York: McGraw-Hill, 1988).

Zimmerman, Paul, *The Los Angeles Dodgers* (New York: Coward-McCann, 1960).

Zimmerman, Tom, "Ballparks of Summers Past," *California Living* (*Los Angeles Herald-Examiner*), March 15, 1987, pp. 1, 6–11.

———, *Working at the Stadium* (Los Angeles: Pacific Tides Press, 1989).

ABOUT THE AUTHOR

Tom Zimmerman is a native of Los Angeles. He is completing his Ph.D. in American History at U.C.L.A., where his dissertation topic is the history of photography in Los Angeles. Zimmerman's word and photo essays have appeared in a number of publications, including the *Los Angeles Times Magazine*, *Americana*, *Condé Nast Traveler*, and *The Journal of the West*. His previous book, published by Pacific Tides in 1989, is *Working at the Stadium*. His photographs have been exhibited across the country, and are in the permanent collections of the Brooklyn Museum, Director's Guild, California Historical Society, and Historic American Building Survey at the National Archives.